MALI

Ettagale Blauer & Jason Lauré

mc Marshall Cavendish
Benchmark
New York

PICTURE CREDITS
Cover photo: © Bruno Morandi/Getty Images
AFP/Getty Images: 38 • AFP: 31, 42 • age fotostock/GEORG GERSTER: 16, 97 • age fotostock/KEVIN O'HARA: 125 • age fotostock/MICHEL RENAUDEAU: 19, 91 • alt.TYPE/reuters: 30, 34, 37, 39, 43, 45, 60, 95, 110 • Audrius Tomonis: 135 • Bruno Morandi/Robert Harding: 107 • Corbis: 11, 32, 36, 51, 57, 63, 65, 78, 83, 84, 109, 114, 115, 119, 127 • Craig Pershouse/Lonely Planet Images: 1 • David Else/Lonely Planet Images: 18, 21, 24 • David Sutherland: 116 • Eye Ubiquitous/ Jamie Carstairs: 64, 117 • Eye Ubiquitous/Hutchison: 17 • Focus Team Italy: 6, 48, 102 • Hutchison/ Christina Dodwell: 12 • Hutchison/ Edward Parker: 62 • Hutchison/ Sarah Errington: 7, 47, 72, 96 • Hutchison/ Stephen Pern: 8 • Hutchison/Mary Jeliffe: 26 • Hutchison/ Tim Beddow: 49 • Jason Laure: 15, 22, 46, 54, 61, 68, 74, 76, 77, 79, 80, 81, 85, 89, 104, 108, 112, 118, 120, 121, 124, 129 • Matt Fletcher/Lonely Planet Images: 50 • Patrick Ben Luke Syder/Lonely Planet Images: 4, 5 • Photolibrary: 3, 10, 13, 14, 35, 52, 55, 56, 58, 59, 66, ,69, 70, 73, 82, 86, 90, 93, 94, 100, 122, 126, 128 • Stockfood/Fotos Mitgeschmack: 130 • Stockfood/Teubner Foodfoto: 131• Thor Vaz de Leon/Lonely Planet Images: 98 • Travel Ink/Getty Images: 99 • Tropix.co.uk/M.Fleetwood: 71 • Tropix.co.uk/V. and M. Birley: 92 • James P. Blair/National Geographic Image Collection: 53

PRECEDING PAGE
Two Malian boys carrying watermelons in Djenne, Mopti.

Publisher (U.S.): Michelle Bisson
Editors: Christine Florie, Stephanie Pee, Louisa Koh
Copyreader: Kristen Azzara
Designer: Rachel Chen
Cover picture researcher: Connie Gardner
Picture researchers: Thomas Khoo, Joshua Ang

Marshall Cavendish Benchmark
99 White Plains Road
Tarrytown, NY 10591
www.marshallcavendish.us

Originated and designed by Times Media Private Limited
An imprint of Marshall Cavendish International (Asia) Private Limited
A member of Times Publishing Limited

All Internet sites were correct and accurate at the time of printing.

Library of Congress Cataloging-in-Publication Data

Blauer, Ettagale.
  Mali / by Ettagale Blauer and Jason Lauré
    p. cm. — (Cultures of the world)
  Summary: "Provides comprehensive information on the geography, history, governmental structure, economy, cultural diversity, peoples, religion, and culture of Mali"—Provided by publisher.
  Includes bibliographical references and index.
  ISBN 978-0-7614-2568-7
1. Mali—Juvenile literature. I. Lauré, Jason. II. Title. III. Series

DT551.22.B58 2007
966.23—dc22   2006101933

Printed in China
7 6 5 4 3 2 1

CONTENTS

A man on a pirogue along the Niger River.

A Dogon man on stilts at the masked Harvest Ceremony in the village of Tirelli.

INTRODUCTION

MALI IS A VAST NATION—the eighth largest in Africa. In the Bambara language, Mali's most widely spoken language, its name means "hippo," though Mali does not have much wildlife. It is often called the crossroads of Africa because great civilizations and empires were born there. Caravans have traveled across Mali on trackless sands, navigating by the stars, guided by centuries of experience. It is a place where history comes alive around every turn in the road. That history is more than 1,000 years old. Mali is home to two fascinating and complex cultures, the Tuareg and the Dogon. Their different ways of life help define the nation of Mali. In many ways they also spell out the history of the region and show how people adapt to extremely difficult climates and geography. They have also survived many periods of foreign rule, including European colonization.

Mali is a new nation, independent only since 1960. The nation has suffered through many political changes, including military and one-party rule. Today, Mali is considered one of the most democratic and peaceful countries in Africa.

GEOGRAPHY

MALI IS A LANDLOCKED COUNTRY that sprawls across northwestern Africa, covering 478,000 square miles (1.2 million sq km). Mali is about the size of Texas and California combined. The country is shaped somewhat like a butterfly tilted to one side. It measures 532 miles (1,500 km) from the north to the south and 1,118 miles (1,800 km) from the easternmost border to the westernmost border. The entire northern half of the country lies within the vast Sahara. The Sahara makes life and travel extremely difficult for those living in Mali. The only permanent settlements there are villages clustered around deep water sources called oases.

South of the Sahara is a shifting region of semidesert. This area is called the Sahel, from the Arabic word meaning "shore." The people who live there see the Sahara as a vast ocean of sand, while the shore is an area that can support life. In the Sahel it is possible to find grazing areas for livestock, which most Malians need to sustain life.

Left: **Cattle grazing in the Sahel. Overgrazing on marginal land like this contributes to desertification, a serious problem in Mali.**

Opposite: **The Sahara desert forms a great part of the Malian landscape.**

In Mali, geography determines how and where people live. When water holes dry up, the people who live in the Sahel move to the south. Some people try to find other areas to graze their livestock, but many are forced to move into towns even farther south. Those who live near the mighty Niger River use its water to irrigate their crops, water livestock, and keep households running. In general, the climate is growing drier, and more and more people are being forced to leave their traditional lands. The rapidly growing population forces people to grow crops in poor soil. This overuse of delicate land leads to further drying of the soil.

The lack of water and arable land force many farmers to cultivate over-grazed soil.

THE SAHARA

The Sahara is a vast ocean of sand that covers almost all of North Africa. It measures about 800 to 1,200 miles (1,300–1,900 km) from north to south and about 3,000 miles (4,800 km) from east to west. It is mainly composed of hard-packed sand and mountains, with rock plains and the occasional oasis. Huge sand dunes are found in isolated areas.

The Sahara has not always been a vast desert. An inland sea once covered the land. When it dried up, the area became a fertile plain. Scientists, viewing rock paintings found in the central Sahara, have shown that people and wildlife lived there, with plenty of grazing land and vegetation. There were many wild animals, including giraffe, elephant, and antelope, as well as herds of cattle. The people living there at the time had a comfortable life, with grassy plains supporting their livestock. Ten thousand years ago this region was green with vegetation. There was a shift in the earth's axis at that time that brought about an increase in both sunshine and rainfall, allowing wild grains to flourish.

About 7,000 years ago the people living in the region began to form permanent settlements. They domesticated sheep to use for food and

SANDSTORMS

When harsh wind blows across the Sahara, it picks up tiny particles of sand and whips them into a sandstorm. This wind, called the harmattan, carries fine, dry sand. It can bring the visibility down to zero and stop people in their tracks. The sky can be clear one moment and then totally obscured the next. The wind-driven sand gets into every tiny crack and crevice. A person who is outside must try to find shelter.

clothing. The rains that fell were absorbed by the earth and created underground reservoirs of water. This is the water that now feeds wells and oases spotted throughout the Sahara.

Over the next several thousand years the climate changed again. A shift in the earth's movement brought less sun and less rain to the area. This region became the desert we now know as the Sahara.

The Sahara is home to nomadic people. For hundreds of years, these people have traveled through this desert and survived.

The Sahara is a growing desert, constantly claiming more land. As the population grows and there are more people with herds of livestock, more grazing land is needed. People have moved their goats and other animals onto land that was once considered marginal, that is land that can barely support any vegetation at all. Once the goats eat all the vegetation, there is nothing to hold the moisture in the land. The land becomes drier and soon gets covered with the sands of the Sahara. North of the town of Ségou, where the desert meets land with some vegetation, one can actually see this shift taking place.

It is not only flat land that is being taken over by the Sahara. About 15 percent of the Sahara consists of dunes. As the wind blows steadily out of the northeast, it pushes the sand up one side of a dune and down the other. It is a slow process, but over time, one can actually see a dune on the move. Travelers who have been coming to the region for 30 or 40 years remember when there were towns that had trees and other vegetation around them that are now completely deserted because the Sahara has moved in.

THE SAHEL

The shift from Sahara to Sahel is an ongoing process. There is no real border between these two regions. In some areas the Sahara is said to be "growing" because it claims more and more land. The Sahel can support some crops, but this is dependent on the rains. In good seasons, when the rains come, farmers can grow food. In poor seasons, when the rains fail, the farmers in this region are unable to grow enough food to sustain their families. In most of the Saharan region of Africa the Sahel is shrinking, making it more difficult for people to find enough food for their livestock. This process is known as desertification. As more and more of the land dries up and becomes part of the Sahara, there is even greater pressure put on the remaining land. In some areas the change is so abrupt that the line that divides the Sahara from the Sahel can actually be seen. In one section the land has a small covering of green, and right next to it, it is covered in a film of fine sand.

Further to the south the savannah region of the country generally has the best climate. This is where most of Mali's people live.

Above: **Herdsmen taking their cattle to graze on the Sahel.**

Opposite: **A nomadic Tuareg on his camel traveling through the Sahara.**

The Bandiagara escarpment, a wedged shaped sandstone cliff where the Dogon build structures into.

MALI'S NEIGHBORS

Mali shares borders with seven countries. Large areas of three of them, Algeria to the north, Niger to the east, and Mauritania to the west, are also part of the Sahara. The other four nations that form Mali's irregular southern border are, from east to west, Burkina Faso, Côte d'Ivoire (Ivory Coast), Guinea, and Senegal. Most of these countries were formerly part of French West Africa. The divisions between them were drawn by the French, who parceled out the land they controlled according to their own bureaucratic needs. This is why the borders between Mali and Algeria, and Mali and Mauritania are so straight.

Some of the land that Mali occupies is extremely flat. It does have two dramatic highland areas that are edged by steep cliffs. The Dogon Plateau, east of the Niger Valley, is bordered by the Bandiagara Escarpment. This separates the Dogon's land from the rest of Mali and has allowed the Dogon to maintain their own culture even though they are located in the geographic center of the country.

SAND BURIES A TOWN

Arouane is a town that has lived through shifting sands. The adobe walls of houses where people used to live can be seen half buried by the sand. Some have tried to save the town by planting gardens, but the blowing desert wind brings in the sand faster than anyone can sweep it out. It is like trying to hold back an ocean with a little pail and shovel.

MOUNTAINS

In the hilly region of the southwest, where Mali borders on Guinea, are the Kéniéba Mountains. These mountains rise to heights of 1,312 to 1,968 feet (400–600 m).

Located in the eastern-central part of the country is the Gandamia Massif, rising 3,543 feet (1,080 m). The highest point in the country, Mount Hombori, 3,789 feet (1,155 m), is found there. Most of the country, about 90 percent of the land consists of plains and plateaus. This flatness plays a very important role in the way rainfall affects the land. By far the most important feature of the center of the country is the Niger River floodplain. It dominates the landscape as well as the life of the nation.

Fatima's Hand, a natural rock formation in the Hombori Mountains lures many adventure tourists to scale its walls.

The Bambouk Mountains, in the extreme western part of the country, run up against the Tambaoura Escarpment. This is next to Mali's border with Senegal. Up in the extreme northeastern corner is a sandstone plateau called the Adrar des Ifoghas. This is the southern end of the Hoggar Mountain Range that dominates southern Algeria.

The lowest elevation is found at the Senegal River, just 75 feet (23 m) above sea level.

THE NIGER RIVER

The Niger River flows across Mali from west to east and supports a major part of the nation's economy and transportation. The river

Pirogues along the Senegal River.

starts to the west, in neighboring Guinea, and flows northeast toward the Sahara. About two-thirds of the way across Mali, it makes a great turn and heads south toward the border with Niger. This turn is known as the Niger Bend.

When the rains are plentiful and the Niger River is full, it helps support life. The river itself and the land on either side of it support many of the food crops grown in Mali.

The word Niger is believed to come from a Berber word, *Gher-N-Igheaen*, which means "river of rivers." It is the third-longest river in Africa, after the Nile and Congo rivers. It runs for a total of 2,600 miles (4,200 km) through West Africa, and 1,050 miles (1,700 km) of that total is found in Mali. Its flow varies according to the time of year and depends on how heavy the seasonal rains are. During the rainy season, which varies through the country but usually occurs some time between July and December, 800 miles (1,300 km) of the river can be navigated. This allows people and goods to travel by boat from town to town. Virtually all of Mali's important towns are found along the path of the Niger River. Seventy-five percent of all the people in Mali live in the region that is crossed by the Niger River.

Although Mali has lost most of its wildlife, it still has very interesting desert-dwelling elephants and manatees that live along and in the Niger River.

Malians fishing on the Niger River with the city of Bamako in the background.

NIGER INLAND DELTA

In the last months of the rainy season, the amount of water in the Niger River increases until it begins to flood its banks and spread out into streams and lagoons. As the water level increases, it covers a vast area of the flat land. This floodplain is known as the Niger Inland Delta. It covers an area measuring 7,722 square miles (20,000 sq km). In the south the rainy season usually runs from October to April. In the north the rainy season may last only from July through September. The farther north, the less rain there is, even during the rainy season.

Whether the rains are heavy or light, the water that flows along the Niger River is greatly reduced during its journey through Mali. It is estimated that almost two-thirds of the flow disappears as it makes

The floodplain known as the Niger Inland Delta is an important area for farming because of its fertile soil.

its journey between Ségou and Timbuktu, a distance of 372 miles (600 km). This happens because the water seeps into the sandy soil and also because of evaporation as it nears the Sahara. Water is also diverted by the Niger Basin Authority for irrigation.

The marshland, with its flow of freshwater, is used to grow rice, millet, and sorghum. Even in the area that is not flooded, the farmers benefit. They carry water to their fields in animal skins.

SENEGAL RIVER

Mali's other important river is the Senegal River, which begins its journey in southwestern Mali. It is formed by two rivers, the Bafing and Bakoye, which meet at the town of Bafoulabé in the westernmost part of Mali. This river flows to the northwest. Its main tributary is the Falémé River, which forms the Senegal-Mali border. The total length of the Senegal River is 1,020 miles (1,641 km). During the rainy season boats can travel along the river as far as Kayes in western Mali. Kayes has a reputation for being

Rice seedlings grow well in the region near the Niger River.

the hottest place in all of Africa. On an average day the high temperature reaches 95°F (35°C), but in April and May the average temperature is 104°F (40°C). The Senegal River also creates a floodplain that is much smaller than that of the Niger River. Rice is grown within the floodplain. River water is also used to irrigate other crops.

CLIMATE

Mali has three seasons. It is generally hot and dry from March to May, warm and rainy from June to October, and cooler and dry from November to February. These seasons vary in different regions of the country, naturally, with the Sahara being hotter and much drier than the savannah.

A cataract of rocks along the Senegal River located near the region of Kayes.

Average temperatures year round are between 80°F and 85°F (27°C–29°C). In April and May temperatures reach 95 to 104°F (35°C–40°C). The hottest period is from March to July, when temperatures often exceed 100°F (38°C). In the Sahara daytime temperatures often rise above 110°F (43°C). At night temperatures in the winter months in the Sahara can plunge as low as 40°F (4°C).

RAINFALL

Rainfall amounts differ greatly throughout the country. In the desert region less than 8 inches (200 mm) fall each year. In the Sahelian region rainfall can range from 8 to 27 inches (200–700 mm) during the year. In the southern grasslands, known as the Sudanic region, rainfall amounts range from 27 to 51 inches (700–1,300 mm) each year.

BAMAKO

Bamako, Mali's capital city, is located on the Niger River in the southwestern corner of the country. More than 1 million people live

Poor farming conditions have forced many rural people to move to the capital city of Bamako.

19

Opposite: **The Grande Marché at Bamako.**

in Bamako, around 10 percent of the population of the entire country. Its population has grown rapidly in recent years as people have left their rural homes. Drought has pushed people off the land, and they often flock to cities looking for work. Bamako began its modern life in 1908, when it became the capital of French Sudan during the colonial era.

Today, Bamako is Mali's most modern city and a very charming place. It combines aspects of its African heritage with a strong touch of French culture, the result of its previous colonization. The Niger River runs right through the city, and there are bridges that connect the northern and southern parts. Thanks to a railway built in the early 1900s, Bamako is Mali's commercial center due to its accessibility and infrastructure. It has an international airport as well as a train and bus station. The city is situated at the foot of the Manding Mountains.

MUSEUMS

There are several museums in Bamako, each with a different way of presenting information about the country and its people. The Musée National (National Museum) shows Mali's history through art, artifacts, and exhibits of Malian textiles, and also shows films about the history and cultures of Mali. The Musée du District de Bamako (Bamako District Museum) opened in December 2003 and also shows some of Mali's history, particularly during the colonial era, but it concentrates more on Bamako itself. The Muso Kunda, or Musée de le Femme (Woman's Museum), focuses on the role of women in Mali. It is a good place to see regional costumes and to sample African food in the museum's restaurant.

MARKETS

At the Grand Marché (main market) the people of Bamako buy their household goods as well as clothing. There are also shops in Bamako where people buy items used in traditional medicine. Many of these items are animal parts that are thought to cure illnesses or to bring luck. They are very expensive for the average Malian, but they are very popular.

MOPTI

The city of Mopti is situated almost exactly in the center of Mali. It is often called the Venice of Africa because it contains a series of dykes and canals that date back several hundred years. It began as a fishing village. Today, it is home to 90,000 people. Mopti is also known as one of the trading centers of Mali because of its important position on Mali's principal river. Mopti has an arts and crafts market where one can find crafts from all over Mali. Here, where pirogues and larger boats dock, all the goods produced in the region as well as imported goods may be found.

Mali is home to the largest mud structure in the world, the Great Mosque.

DJENNÉ

Some of the most historic and mysterious places on the map of the world, including Timbuktu and Djenné, are found in Mali. Though the town of Djenné (jen-NAY) has a small population of just 10,000, it is an extremely important place in Mali and in the Muslim world. It once was known as one of the two most important places of Islamic learning, along with Timbuktu. Yet Djenné is a special place in Mali today because it is the site of a remarkable piece of architecture, the Great Mosque. It is the largest mud, or adobe, structure in the world.

The mosque is also the site of one of the most lively and important markets in Mali. Every Monday thousands of traders and customers gather right in front of the mosque, and a lively exchange begins. This is a market meant for Malians. The goods are household items, not souvenirs, but the market itself is considered a sight worth seeing.

In 1988 Djenné was named a World Heritage Site by the United Nations Educational, Scientific and Cultural Organization (UNESCO). This gives the city the means to preserve, maintain, and protect its ancient buildings. It shows that the entire world recognizes the importance of this town, and that is a great honor for Mali. The United States has contributed funds specifically to help preserve Djenné's important, historic buildings.

BUILDING THE MOSQUE

The Great Mosque was built in 1907 on the foundation of an even older mosque that was built in 1834. That mosque was built on the foundation of one that dates back to even earlier times, the 13th century, when King Koy Konboro, the twenty-sixth ruler of Djenné, converted to Islam and built a mosque. This type of layering is demanded by the Koran itself, which forbids a faithful Muslim from destroying a mosque. If, however, the mosque falls apart because of neglect, the site can be used to build a new mosque. And so it has been in Djenné.

The mosque is enormous and is built from dried bricks that are formed by hand. A wooden frame helps support the mud bricks, but it has another purpose. Every year, at the end of the rainy season, the mosque needs a bit of renovation. The mud must be renewed, and to do this, a maze of ladders and planks are erected using that wooden support. The entire town pitches in to help with the remudding, even people who are not Muslims. As many as 4,000 people play a role in the job. In this way the mosque retains its shape and gives worshippers and tourists a unique and elegant building.

HISTORY

BEFORE THERE WAS A COUNTRY called Mali, there was the Mali Empire. It covered a huge territory that stretched from the coast of West Africa and reached as far east as the modern-day town of Gao, a distance of 1,367 miles (2,000 km). By the end of the 12th century A.D. gold had been discovered in Buré, in what is now Guinea. This made the Mali Empire very rich. Mali also controlled the salt trade. Salt was a vital part of everyday life as it allowed people to preserve food.

EARLY RULERS

The Mali Empire began as a small kingdom made up of the Malinke people. At the time, this kingdom, located around the upper Niger River, was part of the Ghana Empire. The Mali Empire revolted against the rule of the Ghana Empire. Sundjata (Sundiata), a poor, handicapped man who later became the ruler of Mali, was born in Niani near the gold fields of Buré. He had many resources to help him break away from the Ghana Empire. His people had camels, horses, and donkeys, as well as the Niger River. All of these were vital to transporting goods. Their land was fertile, thanks to the Niger River. They were able to grow more food than they needed and to trade this food for other goods.

TIMBUKTU

One thousand years ago the city of Timbuktu rose on the edge of the Sahara. There are at least two stories about the origins of the city's name. One claims that a woman named Buktu brought her herd there to graze. She discovered an oasis, a place in the desert with water and trees. The word tim means water well. Soon, the area became known as Buktu's water well—Timbuktu. But the other story of the name's source contends that it comes from the Songhai language, used throughout West Africa

Opposite: **The ruins of Fort de Medine that was built during French colonial times along the Senegal River near Kayes.**

Present day Timbuktu with irrigated vegetable plots on the outskirts of town.

at that time. The town is located in a slight depression, which in Songhai is called Tombouctou.

The city attracted caravans arriving from the north. They began to stop there to water their camels. Merchants began to set up shops to serve the caravans. While shipments of salt were coming down from the north, shipments of gold were traveling up from the southwest. All of it passed through Timbuktu. By the 15th century the town's population had grown to 100,000, an extraordinary number for that time.

As the business side of the city grew, so too did its religious and intellectual lives. Timbuktu became known as a center of Islamic learning, and part of that was a vibrant publishing industry. Not only were there people to write the books, there were also people who knew how to produce the books, such as leather workers who made the bindings and calligraphers who wrote out the texts. Families created their own libraries, with most of the texts written in Arabic, but many also written in African languages using the Arabic script. The books remained in families, becoming part of the heritage of each new generation. It is estimated that Timbuktu was home to half a million books and manuscripts, many dating back to the 12th century.

THE RULE OF SUNDJATA

Under Sundjata, the tiny kingdom of Mali began to grow. Sundjata took the title Mansa, or King of Kings. He ruled from 1230 until his death in 1255. He was able to control many different areas and peoples. His empire included the goldfields of Buré and Bumbuk, the salt mines of Taghaza, and the important cities of Timbuktu, Djenné, and Gao. Sundjata profited from all the farming activities in the region. He was given tribute, similar to a tax, by people throughout the area. Some of this was in the form of food, and some of it in the form of weapons. Everything that traveled through the empire, every kind of material good, was taxed.

MANSA MUSA

Mali grew even stronger in the next century, during the reign of Kankan Musa, also known as Mansa Musa. He ruled two of the vast regions of the Niger Inland Delta and the important cities of Timbuktu and Gao from 1312 until 1337. Mansa Musa was an exceptionally able ruler. He ruled his vast territory by dividing it into more manageable regions called provinces. He had an army that kept the peace and controlled the profitable trade routes.

During this period Timbuktu reached the height of its glory as a center of learning. Djenné and Gao were also important centers of Islamic studies during this period. They attracted Muslim scholars from distant lands.

PILGRIMAGE TO MECCA

One of the biggest changes that took place during this period of great learning was the introduction of Islam as the religion of the empire's rulers. Islam had been introduced by Muslim traders coming from North Africa. Mansa Musa wanted to show that he was an extremely faithful Muslim. In 1324 he made a pilgrimage to Mecca, the holy city. He did it in an extremely grand style. It is believed that he traveled with 60,000 people, carrying an enormous amount of gold. Along the way he gave away so many gold bars, he caused gold prices to drop in Egypt. The economy there did not recover for ten years.

The Mali Empire's great period came to an end shortly after the death of Mansa Musa. Without the force of his personality and his wise leadership, parts of his empire revolted and became independent. The Tuareg, whose nomadic way of life made them far more difficult to rule

LEARNING FROM THE MANUSCRIPTS

Books were not at the center of learning at this time, but were at the heart of the region's daily life. Elders used the texts to resolve disputes. "The manuscripts talk about everything," according to Abdel Kader Haidara, a member of an ancient Timbuktu family who has inherited his family's impressive collection of books. Some of their collection is 850 years old. "There are copies of the Koran and hadiths (sayings of the prophet Muhammad) as well as sermons and explanations of Islamic law. The books also discuss astronomy, mathematics, medicine, and geography. There are manuscripts of contracts, commercial records, and decrees that show how conflicts were resolved. They are changing the way people think about Africa, and Africans, because they prove that there was a literate culture in place a long time ago. Even though Timbuktu lost its position as a place of scholarly learning, its history was just waiting to be discovered by the outside world."

FATHER OF MALI

In the late 17th century a man was born who was known as Bitòn or Mamary Coulibaly. He is credited with founding the Bambara Empire in Ségou, where he became head of the Tòn, an organization for young men. With that group he overpowered other chiefs in the region and established the Bambara Empire. His army was enormous for the time. It is estimated that he had 1,000 men as well as war canoes to fight his battles and patrol the Niger River. Coulibaly paid for these adventures through the slave trade. He traded human beings to get the weapons and equipment he needed. His empire only survived for ten years after his death in 1766.

than the settled farmers, rebelled against the government. They raided Timbuktu, which was in the northernmost reaches of the empire. By the mid-15th century the Mali Empire had been taken over by the Songhai Empire already established around Gao. Then the land was invaded by the Moroccan army from the north in 1590. Although the Moroccans broke up the existing government, they were not able to rule such an enormous area. Their homeland, in the north of Africa, was separated from Mali by the forbidding Sahara.

FRENCH GAIN CONTROL

At the end of the 18th century, the region was left on its own, with no central government. Without strong leaders its prosperous years ended. Smaller, regional kingdoms arose, including the Bambara kingdoms of Ségou and Kaarta, a Peul (Peulh) kingdom in the Niger Inland Delta, and several others. During the 19th century a battle for control was being staged by the French and two Muslim-controlled empires. In order to defeat the local Mali leaders, the French brought in the French Foreign Legion. This legion was made up entirely of foreigners, not Frenchmen, who were paid to fight foreign wars. France used the legion throughout the Sahara to conduct its wars. By 1898 the French had gained total control of a vast region in West Africa. Mali, known then as French Sudan, was incorporated into French West Africa.

French president Jacques Chiraq (*left*) and Mali's Amadou Toumani Toure at the 2007 French-African Summit in Cannes. The French and Malians continue to have close ties despite the end of colonial rule.

FRENCH WEST AFRICA

The French colonial period was marked by two different ways of governing. At the beginning of the 20th century the French tried a policy of assimilation. This encouraged Africans to be educated in French culture so they would be more closely tied to France, the mother country. This shifted to a policy called association in which the Africans were encouraged to merge their own culture with French culture and ultimately become European in their way of thinking. The introduction of the French language had a long-lasting effect. To this day French is the official language of Mali. However, the Bambara language is widely used as well.

OPPOSITION GROWS

Over the next 60 years, the French ruled this region as one unit. Its control included eight territories in addition to Mali: Dahomey, now the nation of Benin; French Guinea (now called Guinea); Cote d'Ivoire, Mauritania, Niger, Senegal, and Upper Volta (now the nation of Burkina Faso). This entire region was ruled by a governor-general. Between World War I and World War II opposition to French colonial rule grew. This opposition was nurtured in trade unions. These organizations, especially the teachers' union, gave Malians a place to meet and exchange views. One of the most important of these was the Sudanese Union, led by Modibo Keita, who would lead Mali to independence.

MODIBO KEITA

Modibo Keita was descended from the emperors of Mali. He had radical ideas about how Mali should be governed. He created a nation patterned after the ideas of the Soviet Union, which was then a powerful political force. He took Mali out of the West African Economic and Monetary Union in 1962 and introduced a new currency called the Mali Franc. This meant that Mali was not able to trade with any other nation because no one else accepted its money. Traders were unable to deal with the merchants of the neighboring African countries, their primary source of income. Not surprisingly, the people revolted against this move. In response Keita brought in a militia to restore order and to eliminate political opposition to his rule.

Keita was also opposed by the fierce Tuareg, the nomads who roamed the Sahara. In 1963 he used his own military force to defeat the Tuareg. Though they have little political power, the Tuareg have become a symbol of freedom. With their camels and their ability to survive in the Sahara, they are a people who feel no ties to any nation. They remain true to their own way of life.

INDEPENDENCE

French control ended in 1960, when the region now called the Republic of Mali became fully independent. Its first president was Modibo Keita. He immediately set about steering Mali on a dramatically different course. He believed in socialism, a system in which the government directs the economy. He ruled by military force, pushing forward his policies. Because of these policies the economy declined. There were shortages of consumer products, especially food. Within a few years he had no choice but to make a deal with France, the former colonial ruler, to accept aid if he changed his policies. His own political party members were furious about this and tried to force the people to accept their socialist policies. Most Malians were against them. The military officers themselves, who were being used to enforce the policies, soon revolted. In 1968, while Keita was out of the capital city of Bamako, they staged a bloodless coup. They seized power from the government and arrested Keita when he tried to return. This coup was headed by Moussa Traoré, a lieutenant in the army.

MILITARY RULE

Moussa Traoré (*left*) pictured with the president of Chad, Hissène Habré (1982–90).

Unfortunately for Mali, Traoré set about ruling the country as he saw fit and established a military-run government. Although he had come into office with a promise to return the country to civilian rule, he used his

power to remove opponents to his military rule. He made sure that he and his party, the Comité Militaire de Libération Nationale (CMLN), remained in power, running the country under the military.

TURMOIL IN MALI

Throughout the rest of the 1970s and 1980s, Traoré clung to power. His government was marked by corruption and a huge number of people had been given jobs in the government just to keep them on his side. A drought in 1984 put even greater economic pressure on the country as crops failed. Protests against the government and its policies continued to grow, led by students and trade union members. In 1991 the military put down a protest, killing 106 people. The next day Traoré was thrown out of power very much the way he came into it, through a coup led by a military man, Lieutenant Colonel Amadou Toumani Touré. Touré is known

TUAREGS RETURN

During a drought in the 1970s many Tuaregs had taken refuge in Algeria and Libya. When they began to return to Mali in the 1980s by the thousands, they brought with them military skills and weapons. In 1990 they came into conflict with the Malian army at Menana. Fierce fighting broke out. The Tuareg wanted to create an independent region of the desert that included Timbuktu. Tension and skirmishes continued even as a series of peace treaties were signed between the Tuareg and the governments of Mali and other neighboring nations. By 1995 the peace process had moved forward, and the fighters were turning in their weapons. In a symbolic gesture to show that the fighting was over, weapons were burned at the Flame of Peace in Timbuktu on March 27, 1996. To remember that event, a monument was built from burned AK-47 rifles. They were buried in cement to show that the fighting was truly over. Although the monument is not considered beautiful, the destruction of the rifles reassures the local people and makes a powerful political statement.

as the "soldier of democracy" because he turned the government over to the people after he ended the military dictatorship, which led the way to a multiparty democracy and Mali's first democratically elected president, Alpha Oumar Konaré. Konaré remained in power until 2002, when he lost to Amadou Touré.

MODERN DEMOCRACY

Today, Mali is considered a model of democracy and a shining light in Africa. It is a nation at peace. In spite of ethnic differences between its peoples, it does not experience any fighting. Thanks to the discovery of gold deposits that are large enough to be worked on a commercial basis, its economy has improved dramatically. This, in turn, has led to an increase in tourism, which adds to the economy. Most of the tourists go to see historic Djenné and Timbuktu and to experience the great living cultures of the Tuareg and the Dogon people.

PEACE CORPS

Many visitors to Mali came as Peace Corps workers. In 1960 John F. Kennedy was campaigning for the presidency of the United States. When he arrived at the University of Michigan, he made a speech that electrified the students and ultimately led to the formation of the program called the Peace Corps. In his speech he challenged students to "serve the cause of peace" by living and working in developing countries. Students as well as older adults enthusiastically took up his challenge, devoting two years of their lives to the program.

Alpha Oumar Konaré was the president of Mali for two consecutive terms (1992–2002). He worked at restoring democracy to Mali.

The Peace Corps program began in Mali in 1971. Nearly 2,000 Peace Corps volunteers have served in the program in Mali since then. The program in Mali is one of the largest Peace Corps programs in Africa. Currently, 180 people are working there. They work in many different areas of development. Their goal is to establish programs the Malians can continue on their own when the volunteers leave. These programs include food production, water availability, environmental conservation, small-business development, and preventive health care, including HIV/AIDS awareness.

Peace Corps volunteers work with the local people, showing by example and adopting their American know-how to the needs of the

Peace Corp volunteers often live among the communities that they serve.

local communities. They make an effort to learn the language in the local area where they are working.

In the area of health needs they work with local health-care providers and community members to improve nutrition and child care. They also encourage ways to control one of the biggest killers of children in Mali, diarrhea. This condition is often caused by drinking dirty water and is a major challenge in many developing countries.

U.S. SOLDIERS IN THE SAHARA

In 2006 the northernmost part of Mali was too dangerous to travel in. The U.S. embassy in Mali advised tourists not to travel to Essakane for a music

Opposite: **A child receiving medical attention from a medic of the U.S. Armed Forces in the village of Tacharane near Gao.**

Below: **The U.S. Special Forces training locals in anti-terror warfar.**

festival. The reason was the presence of U.S. Special Forces. They were sent there by President George W. Bush to train the Malian military on patrol in the vast Sahara north of Timbuktu. It is believed that Islamic terrorist groups saw the barely populated region as a good place to recruit people to its cause. The United States saw stopping this recruitment as a vital part of its global program to combat terrorism and to prevent Al-Qaeda from establishing a base there. Unfortunately, there are many young men with little or no education and no chance of employment who can be won over with money and a promise that they are fighting a worthwhile cause. The kind of militant and strict Islam being promoted by these groups is far from the Islam practiced by most Malians.

PEACEFUL TRANSITION

With the improvements in the economy, thanks to gold mining and tourism, there is great hope in Mali. Jobs are being created, and education is improving. In 2007 the country held its democratic elections for a president and members of parliament. Its recent history shows that it has wise leadership. Mali should remain a shining example of an African nation staying true to its culture while embracing democracy.

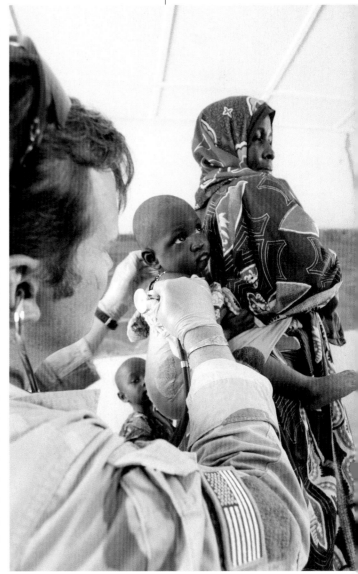

GOVERNMENT

MALI BEGAN ITS LIFE AS A democracy in 1992, when a transitional government was formed to draft a new constitution. The constitution spells out the structure of the new democratic government. It provides for the separation of powers among three branches: executive, legislative, and judicial.

In many new democracies there is a rush to create new political parties. In Mali dozens of political parties took part in the elections. Sixteen of them were successful in gaining seats in the National Assembly. Several parties formed coalitions, using their combined political power to work for change in Mali. The Rally for Mali (Rassemblement Pour le Mali—RPM), the parties in the Hope 2002 coalition (Espoir 2002), and the Alliance for Democracy in Mali party (Allliance pour la Démocratie au Mali—Adema) were the biggest vote-getters.

Left: **President Amadou Toumani Touré (2002–) waves at Malians at an election rally at Bamako.**

Opposite: **A Malian woman casts her vote for Mali's president in the 2007 election.**

NATIONAL ANTHEM

Seydou Badian Kouyaté, a politican and novelist, composed Mali's national anthem, *Pour l'Afrique et pour toi, Mali* (*For Africa and for you, Mali*). It was written in French.

FRENCH LYRICS

A ton appel Mali
Pour ta prospérité
Fidèle à ton destin
Nous serons tous unis
Un peuple, un but, une foi
Pour une Afrique unie
Si l'ennemi découvre son front
Au dedans ou au dehors
Debout sur les remparts
Nous sommes résolus de mourir

CHORUS:
Pour l'Afrique et pour toi Mali
Notre drapeau sera liberté
Pour l'Afrique et pour toi Mali
Notre combat sera unité
Ô Mali d'aujourd'hui
Ô Mali de demain
Les champs fleurissent d'espérance
Les coeurs vibrent de confiance

L'Afrique se lève enfin
Saluons ce jour nouveau
Saluons la liberté
Marchons vers l'unité
Dignité retrouvée
Soutient notre combat
Fidèle à notre serment
De faire l'Afrique unie
Ensemble debout mes frères
Tous au rendez-vous de l'honneur

CHORUS

Debout villes et campagnes
Debout femmes, jeunes et vieux
Pour la patrie en marche
Vers l'avenir radieux
Pour notre dignité
Renforçons bien nos rangs
Pour le salut public
Forgeons le bien commun
Ensemble au coude à coude
Faisons le sentier du bonheur

CHORUS

La voie est dure très dure
Qui mène au bonheur commun
Courage et dévouement
Vigilance à tout moment
Vérité des temps anciens
Vérité de tous les jours
Le bonheur par le labeur
Fera le Mali de demain

CHORUS

ENGLISH TRANSLATION

At your call, Mali,
So that you may prosper,
Faithful to your destiny,
We shall all be united,
One people, one goal, one faith
For a united Africa.
If the enemy should show himself
Within or without,
On the ramparts,
We are ready to stand and die.

CHORUS:
For Africa and for you, Mali,
Our banner shall be liberty.
For Africa and for you, Mali,
Our fight shall be for unity.
Oh, Mali of today,
Oh, Mali of tomorrow,
The fields are flowering with hope
And hearts are thrilling with confidence.

Africa is at last arising,
Let us greet this new day.
Let us greet freedom,
Let us march toward unity.
Refound dignity
Supports our struggle.
Faithful to our oath
To make a united Africa,
Together, arise, my brothers,
All to the place where honor calls.

CHORUS

Stand up, towns and countryside,
Stand up, women, stand up young and old,
For the Fatherland on the road

Toward a radiant future.
For the sake of our dignity
Let us strengthen our ranks;
For the public well-being
Let us forge the common good.
Together, shoulder to shoulder,
Let us work for happiness.

CHORUS

The road is hard, very hard,
That leads to common happiness.
Courage and devotion,
Constant vigilance,
Courage and devotion,
Constant vigilance,
Truth from olden times,
The truths of every day,
Happiness through effort
Will build the Mali of tomorrow.

CHORUS

FORM OF GOVERNMENT

Mali is a republic headed by a president, who is the chief of state. The current president is Amadou Toumani Touré, who has been in power since June 8, 2002. The prime minister is the head of government and is appointed by the president. The prime minister is Ousmane Issoufi Maiga, in power since April 30, 2004. A cabinet of ministers is appointed by the prime minister. As of July 2004 there were 26 cabinet ministers.

THREE BRANCHES OF GOVERNMENT

The executive branch consists of the president, the prime minister, and the cabinet. The president is elected for a five-year term, with a two-term limit. The president's powers are similar to those of the U.S. president. He is the chief of state and commander-in-chief of the country's armed forces.

The legislative branch has one house with 147 seats, called the National Assembly. Its members serve five-year terms. The legislature writes the laws that govern the nation.

Above: **Prime minister of Mali, Ousmane Issoufi Maiga (*right*).**

Opposite: **A man collects his ballot form from an election official in Bamako.**

The judicial branch is the third branch of the government. The Ministry of Justice is responsible for appointing judges and supervising law enforcement. The Supreme Court has judicial as well as administrative powers, ensuring that the laws are carried out properly. The country's legal system combines two very different legal systems together. Its main laws were inherited from France during the colonial period. Its other laws are based on ancient and deep-rooted tribal traditions. In the French civil law system written laws are very specific. Judges make the final decisions in cases. The law is based on the Napoleonic Code and was set down in 1804. It was created originally to make laws clearer and to give ordinary people power. It was a reaction to the power of monarchs who ruled according to their own interests. The newly written laws made it possible for people to be treated more fairly. However, the code established the principle that a person was presumed guilty until proven innocent if the person was arrested by the state. It also established the idea that all male citizens were equal in the eyes of the law. Women were not considered equal to men. Fathers and husbands ruled over their children and wives.

Common law is based on custom or tradition. It grows out of experience and can be more democratic. In common law people often talk their way through the known facts of a case and come to a decision that is most fair to all the people involved. Common or traditional law also takes into consideration the tribal beliefs and practices of each group. It recognizes that in small village settings,

it is important to come to a settlement that people can live with. It is, in many ways, more personal than the formal French code of laws.

The country is divided into eight administrative regions: Gao, Kayes, Kidal, Koulikoro, Mopti, Ségou, Sikasso, and Timbuktu, plus the capital, Bamako.

Mali gained its independence from France on September 22, 1960, and September 22 is a national holiday. This is an exciting event in Mali, marked with parades and political speeches. It marks the day that Mali broke away from a colonial power and became a nation. The country adopted its constitution on January 12, 1992.

The country's flag has three vertical bands of color—green, yellow, and red. These colors were chosen to represent three aspects of Mali. Green symbolizes nature and agriculture. Yellow represents gold, the wealth of the nation, and red symbolizing the sacrifices made to gain independence. These are the traditional colors of the African freedom movement.

ELECTION WATCHERS

Because Mali is still considered a young democracy, independent election observers were present during the election. The Carter Center, headed by the former U.S. president Jimmy Carter, took part in this process and reported on the election. In general, the Carter Center found the elections to be "peaceful, tolerant and competitive." They concluded "The winning candidate, Amadou Toumani Touré appears to enjoy legitimacy in the eyes of the Malian electorate and the international community."

Voter participation was very low. Only 38 percent of registered voters took part in the first round. That fell to just 30 percent in the second round.

AMADOU TOUMANI TOURÉ

President Amadou Toumani Touré was born on November 4, 1948, in Mopti. He studied to become a teacher but joined the army and became a commander. In 1991 he took part in a coup d'etat, which is to overthrow the government by military means, to defeat Moussa Traoré. He became the head of state during this period, leading up to democratic rule. In June 2001 he served as a special envoy of UN Secretary General Kofi Annan to the Central African Republic. Later that year he retired from the army. He ran for president of Mali in 2002 and received 64 percent of the vote in the second runoff election. President Touré is a very unusual political figure. He is not a member of any political party. His government is not a one-party government but has representatives from many Malian political parties.

ELECTIONS

Mali has enjoyed a democratic government since 1992, when multiparty elections became the rule. The elections in 2002 were considered generally free and fair. There was tremendous competition for the presidency. Candidates from 36 political parties as well as many coalition parties were represented.

Each voter was given 24 separate ballot papers representing all of those competing groups. Mali uses a two-round election system. In the first round all of the parties are represented. If no one party gets a majority of the votes, then a second round of voting is needed. With so many parties competing for votes, there is rarely one party with a majority of the votes. In the second round, however, only the two top vote-getters compete.

The presidential election was held in 2007, with Amadou Toumani Touré re-elected as the president of Mali. The National Assembly election was also held in 2007.

ECONOMY

FOR MALI, A NATION IN WHICH most people live in rural areas, farming is the most important industry. Three-quarters of the people depend on agriculture to survive. For farmers the single most important cash crop is cotton. A cash crop is one that is produced to earn money by selling it outside the country. Food crops are usually grown to feed one's own family. The surplus may be sold in a local market. It is estimated that one-third of the entire population works at growing or processing cotton.

BASIC FARMING

Growing cotton is very hard work, especially if one farms the way most Malian farmers do. They plow their fields using donkeys and then plant the seeds. Then they wait for the rains to come. They pray, perform dances, and then pray to the gods once more to send just the

Left: A Malian woman sowing seeds.

Opposite: **An onion field in Dogon. The Dogon depend on the sale of onions for their livelihoods.**

right amount of rain. The farmers hope they will not get too much rain, which can drown the young plants. The farmers also hope the sun will not be too strong and burn the plants. The farmers hope the pesticides they use will keep the boll weevils from eating up the cotton bolls before they are ready to pick.

After all this, if everything goes just right, they pick the cotton by hand, because they cannot afford expensive equipment to do the job. They can barely afford to buy the seeds each year to start the planting process.

A Malian man weaving cotton into cloth to sell. Despite the hard work involved in making cotton, many Malians can barely survive on the income earned from its sale.

INCOME FROM COTTON

Cotton has earned as much as $200 million a year for Mali's economy, although this figure is going down. In the 2004–2005 growing season cotton production was 600,000 tons. The biggest problem Mali's cotton farmers face comes from countries such as the United States. In the United States farmers are given subsidies, or money from the government, for the cotton they produce. This means that even though it costs more for U.S. farmers to grow their cotton than it does for Mali's farmers to grow theirs, the farmers in the United States earn more. The price of cotton produced by U.S. farmers is guaranteed by the U.S. government, which pays them the subsidy. This subsidy for U.S. farmers does not depend on world cotton prices. The U.S. farmers do not have to worry about the price of cotton sold in the marketplace. As a result Mali's farmers are now actually losing money by growing cotton.

From about 1996 to 2006 the United States more than doubled its sales of cotton, even though the world cotton price dropped by more than 50 percent. U.S. farmers could afford to do this because of the subsidy from the U.S. government. The government in Mali cannot afford to subsidize its farmers, who often earn less for their cotton than it costs them to grow it. Although the United States gives a lot of financial aid to Mali, this loss of cotton income keeps the farmers from ever getting ahead.

FARMS ON THE NIGER

Water is the most important resource for farmers. In Mali, where the rain comes only during one season and sometimes does not come at all, it is not surprising that the best area for farming is along the banks of the Niger River. The best farmland is next to the Niger River, between Bamako, the capital, and Mopti. There is also good farming in the southernmost part of the country, in the region where Mali meets the neighboring countries of Guinea, Cote d'Ivoire, and Burkina Faso. There, in addition to cotton and tobacco, food crops such as rice, millet, corn, and other vegetables are grown.

As the Niger floods the land, it brings rich soil with it. This is vital for the farmers. The river is so full of soil, it has a nickname. It is called the "strong brown god." The brown refers to the soil mixed with the water. It is called a god because it brings life back to the dry land. In years when the rains fail, life becomes very difficult for the Malian people. Crops dry up, and livestock die. The people have

Plots of land along the Niger River are used for farming.

The spillway of the hydroelectric dam located at Manantan.

to depend on food aid and hope the next year brings better rains. When the rains fail, as they did in 2005, crops fail, too. An estimated 1 million people needed food aid that year.

Sorghum, wheat, and peanuts are also important crops for Mali. Peanuts are grown in many parts of West Africa and are an important ingredient in stews and other dishes.

DAMMING THE RIVER

Several dams have been built to control the flow of the Niger River. This allows officials to regulate the flow of water throughout the year. Two of these dams are located at Sotuba, near Bamako, and at Markala, near Ségou. Both dams are used to irrigate the local area. This allows farmers to grow crops without depending so much on the annual rains. Even with the dams, however, farmers and all the people must still worry about the drought years, when the rains fail to come.

FISHING

The fishing industry also benefits from the annual flooding. Fish, including the Nile perch, use the marshlands as their spawning grounds. At the end of the rainy season the waters that have covered the floodplain start to recede. The fish do not have enough water to swim in and are easily caught by the fishers. The Niger River itself is a great source of fish.

LIVESTOCK

For many people in Africa wealth is counted in terms of livestock, especially cattle. People who have cattle have something better than money in the bank. They have something that can be eaten or sold to buy other goods. They have something that can multiply on its own and bring them greater wealth. For these reasons, when a family loses some or all of its cattle, it is a catastrophe.

In good years, when the rains come on time, there are millions of cattle, sheep, and goats in Mali. Since the early 1970s, however, Mali has suffered two terrible droughts, and each time, millions of head of livestock died. During the drought that began in 1972 and lasted until 1974, it is estimated that 40 percent of all the livestock in Mali died. The herds started to increase again in the late 1970s, but another drought hit in 1983 and lasted until 1985. Once again the herds were drastically reduced in size. Both of these droughts reduced the area in which cattle can be grazed, and many herders have given up entirely on keeping cattle. Most of the remaining livestock are

A Fulani herder with his cattle. Cattle can be considered more important than money in that they can be eaten or exchanged for other goods.

found in the Niger Inland Delta and in grazing lands to the north of the delta.

The overall size of Mali's herds is not expected to reach predrought levels in the north of the country, where the encroachment of the desert has depleted the grazing region. The largest concentrations of cattle are in the areas north of Bamako and Ségou, extending into the Niger Delta, but herding activity is gradually shifting southward, due to the effects of previous droughts.

Cattle are a small but important part of the economy, making up about 5 percent of exports. They are important because they can be used in place of money to trade for other goods.

Smaller animals that survive in the driest areas, such as sheep, goats, and camels, are raised in the regions north and east of Timbuktu. Camels are known as the "ships of the desert" because they are able to travel vast distances under the most difficult conditions without needing water.

Salt slabs before they are loaded onto camels.

SALT CARAVANS

Mali remains a country in which ancient traditions continue, even in the 21st century. Camel caravans still cross the forbidding sands of the Sahara to reach the salt mines at Taoudenni in the northernmost part of Mali. There, more than 400 miles (645 km) north of Timbuktu, deep in the Sahara, men cut salt blocks from the ancient lake bed where it was formed. The workers are the Bella people, a tribe who were formerly held as slaves by the Tuaregs. Although free today, they continue to do this extremely hard work. They live at the mine and work in unimaginable

heat. They dig the salt out in large slabs that weigh 110 pounds (50 kg) each. Many have been working for the same Tuareg family for generations and do not know any other way to live or work.

A camel caravan in the Sahara. Camel caravans have been used by Malians to transport goods across the desert for a long time.

CAMEL CARAVAN

When the camel caravan arrives, the salt is loaded onto the camels. Four slabs, a total of 440 pounds (200 kg), are loaded onto each camel for the 14-day trip to Timbuktu. A caravan may be made up of hundreds of camels traveling together. They generally travel from October to March, traveling at night because the temperature in the desert can drop 40 degrees from day to night. At the end of each night's ride the camels are unloaded and allowed to rest during the heat of the day. The next evening everything is loaded onto the camels again. The Tuareg or Maur person who leads the camel caravan has a vast knowledge of the desert. He can read the sands the way others read a printed road map. The entire caravan of men and camels place their lives in his hands and in his knowledge of the terrain.

He must know exactly where the next water hole is to be found, because in the desert a mistake can be deadly. When there are no physical features such as rivers, mountains, streets, or buildings to help a person judge where he is going, it is very easy to make a mistake.

SELLING THE SALT

When the caravan arrives in Timbuktu, the salt slabs are loaded onto boats for the trip to Mopti on the Niger River. At Mopti the salt is cut into smaller sections and placed in warehouses. From there it is distributed all over West Africa. At Mopti there is a lively scene as the salt-laden boats arrive. Young women, many from the Bella tribe, carry trays of prepared food that they hope to sell to the boatmen and their passengers.

GOLD

It has been almost 1,000 years since Mali was known as a center of gold mining. In modern times gold has been mined by thousands of individual miners using traditional gold-panning methods. There are several hundred gold deposits in Mali, and these miners work small deposits that do not require industrial equipment. Even small amounts add up. It is estimated that these miners produce more than 2 tons of gold each year.

BIG GOLD DEPOSITS

Although industrial mining began in the 1970s, it was not until the 1980s that major gold deposits were discovered. By the 1990s gold mining in Mali had become a large-scale operation. It was around that time that surveys showed major gold deposits that could be worked profitably by large-scale mining methods. Between 1996 and 1997 gold production in Mali grew from 6.6 tons to 18.5 tons. Today, Mali is the third-largest producer in Africa. Only South Africa and Ghana produce more. In 2003 Mali produced 51.6 tons of gold. This was actually down from 2002, when it produced 63.69 tons. Gold production will grow according to the world gold price. It should remain fairly stable at between 55 and 60 tons per year.

Above: **A worker pans for gold near Essakane.**

Opposite: **Slabs of salt at the port of Timbuktu waiting to be transported down the Niger River.**

Estimates of Mali's gold reserves vary widely, depending on which expert one asks. Some say Mali has 350 tons of gold reserves, while others believe the figure is as high as 500 tons. This does not mean all this gold will be mined. Some of it may be too far underground to work, and some of it may be scattered over such a wide area that it is not profitable to extract. But it does mean that Mali has a tremendous natural resource that could improve the country's economy. This recent upsurge in gold mining has given the economy a much-needed boost. This should help the government improve living conditions as well as education.

GOLD-MINING AREAS

The gold-mining areas are located in the southwestern and southern parts of the country, at Bougouni and Kéniéba, near the countries of Senegal and Guinea. The gold is found within rocks, spread over large areas of land. Some of it is deep within the earth, and some of it is relatively close to the surface. In order to extract the gold, the mining companies must first dig up tons of gold-bearing ore. Some of the mines are called open-pit mines because they are worked from the surface.

The miners scoop up the ore using heavy earth-moving equipment and take it to a processing plant. They make a huge circle in the ground and when they have scooped up all the ore in that circle, they move to the next level down. As they go deeper and deeper into the earth, the circle becomes smaller, like an ice cream cone. Eventually it becomes too small to work this way. At that point the mining company has to decide whether it would be profitable to sink a mine shaft into the earth and begin working the deposit as an underground

A gold mine near Essakane. Despite being the third largest producer of gold in Africa, many Malians still live in poverty.

mine. This is much more expensive, and not all gold deposits are worth it. It is difficult to imagine just how big a new mine pit can be. The Sadiola mine in the western part of Mali, for example, measures 5,900 feet (1,800 m) long by 2,460 feet (750 m) wide. It already produces around 600,000 ounces (23 tons) of gold in a good year. The mine must process 4 million tons of ore in the treatment plant to produce that amount of gold. This mine has gold reserves estimated at 120 tons and is expected to produce an average of 10 tons of gold a year. That means it has a life expectancy of only 12 years.

THE PRICE OF GOLD

Why are gold-mining companies interested in Mali right now? After all, the gold has just been sitting there for centuries. The answer is simple. Gold is sold at a fixed price around the world. That means a miner gets the same price for an ounce of gold, no matter how much work he or she has to do getting it out

A gold miner in Mali.

of the ground. The amount it costs to get the gold out stays pretty much the same for the mining company. So, when the fixed price is low, there is no reason for the company to invest in the mine. But when the world price goes up for whatever reason, the mining company makes more money for that same ounce of gold. In 2006 the price of gold soared to more than $600 per ounce, giving the miners a bigger return on their investment. It also gave Mali income, since the government has a 20 percent share in the mines.

A man weighing gold nuggets.

CHANGING MINING LAWS

In order to allow the gold-mining industry to succeed, the government of Mali had to make major changes to its own rules and regulations. Before the current gold rush the government owned almost all the mining operations in the country. But it did not have the money or the mining know-how to extract much of the gold that was in the ground. In order to bring in new revenue, equipment, and mining engineers, the government agreed that it would only own 20 percent of any mining operations that were set up by outside companies.

The government also gave mining companies great economic incentives to start working in Mali. For example, mining companies do not have to pay any corporate tax for the first five years a mine is in production.

Although Mali's economy has benefited from the gold mining, that does not mean all the people of Mali are wealthier. The mines create environmental problems, too. The gold ore must be processed using cyanide, an extremely harsh chemical. The process also uses a lot of water, and that can be a major problem in a country where there is often too little water for farming.

GENERATING POWER

Water is also vital for the production of hydroelectric power. To create power, a river must first be dammed, creating reservoirs. Mali has three such dams used for irrigation, energy creation, and flood control. The two that are used to create hydroelectric power are the Sélingué Dam, built on the Sankarani River, and the Manantali Dam, on the Bafing River. The energy that is produced is used almost entirely by industry. Very few homes in Mali have access to electricity.

OTHER INDUSTRIES

Mali has a number of small businesses that make products for local use. There is a soft-drink plant, a shoe factory, a flour mill, and a furniture plant. There are companies that make tiles, paint, farm implements, ceramics, and cement. Others are involved in sugar distilling, cottonseed oil production, and meat processing.

Traditionally, most of the wage-paying work has been done by men. Women mainly worked in the home. This is slowly changing as more people move into cities. However, people are moving into the cities faster than jobs can be created.

Unemployed young men. Many feel that a brighter future awaits them outside the borders of Mali.

LEAVING MALI

For people who are looking for employment, there are simply not enough jobs to go around. In Mali, unlike the United States and other countries, there is no welfare system to help support people who cannot find work.

59

A fence decorated with figures to signify the attempt by immigrants to cross the border between Morocco and the Spanish enclave of Melilla.

For a growing number of young men the solution seems to lie outside the country. They feel that if they can reach a European country, they will find work. But this is far from a simple task. They face two major hurdles. First, they do not have money to buy an airline ticket to take them out of the country. But even more importantly, they do not have visas to allow them to enter another country legally. In spite of that, many leave anyway, traveling by extremely difficult routes to try to reach Europe, especially Spain. Although it would make more sense to try to get to France, because many Malians speak French, there is more farmwork available in southern Spain.

They walk and try to hitch rides that take them to the coast of Africa in Morocco. There are two tiny parts of Morocco that still belong to Spain. These are the enclaves of Ceuta and Melilla. An enclave is a small piece of land surrounded by another country. During the colonial period these pieces of land were fought over by European powers. For an African who wants to get to Spain, the first step is to reach Ceuta or Melilla. If he can step onto one of those tiny bits of land, he has officially entered Spain. But his troubles have not ended. In a way they have just begun. This is where the most dangerous part of the journey begins. Now he must try to cross the Mediterranean Sea. Many people die in the attempt. Many others are caught and jailed before being returned to their home country. The Malians do not carry any official documents with them, such as passports, because they do not want the Spanish to know where they came from. They do this to try to avoid being sent back.

TRANSPORTATION

Mali's transportation system is very limited. Most goods, including salt exports as well as locally used products are shipped on boats on the Niger River. There are about 11,000 miles (18,500 km) of road but only about 26 percent are paved. These roads connect the major cities in Mali. Mali has a railroad that connects Bamako, the capital, with Dakar, the capital of Senegal. It is used for both passengers and freight. Modern courier services have set up business in Mali, including DHL, a worldwide carrier of packages and documents.

An overcrowded piroque on the Niger River. Much of Mali's transportation is dependent on the Niger River.

Because there is a lack of telephone networks in most of Mali, more people depend on cell phones than on traditional landlines. While there were only 74,900 landline telephones in use in 2004, there were 400,000 cell phones. Few people own television sets, but there are more than half a million radios in use, and that is how most people get their news, information, and entertainment. There are more radio broadcasting stations in Mali than in any other African nation, offering 250 programs.

Some radios work on batteries and do not depend on electricity. Most people outside the main cities do not have access to electricity, although some have small generators. Some jobs are created through the sale of cell phones and providing cell phone services. Even selling batteries can provide employment. Many people set up small stands on the street, selling small quantities of batteries as well as food, clothes, and other basic goods. This is called casual employment. It does not offer much of a future, but for many people, it is the only kind of work they can find.

ENVIRONMENT

THE NATURAL ENVIRONMENT IS SOMETHING that guides every day of every person's life in Mali. No one needs to tell the people of Mali about global warming. They can see the Sahara advancing through their communities. The problem was so severe in the late 1960s and early 1970s that it made news around the world. The result was a conference held by the United Nations on the subject of desertification, through which the desert is claiming more land. This is Mali's chief environmental concern. Generally, once the Sahara claims land, it does not give it back. So after a drought is over, there is a loss of inhabitable land. This puts a strain on the remaining land. The extreme heat and dryness of the Sahara makes the lands nearby drier and less able to support agriculture and livestock.

Although a few years of good rains made life easier in the 1980s, the general trend is toward a drier climate. A drier climate means a loss of farmland. At

Left: **A shepherd watching over his cattle. Overgrazing is one of the causes of Mali's loss of arable land.**

Opposite: **Acacia trees and millet stubble spotting the plain fronting the Bandiagara escarpment.**

the same time Mali's rapidly growing population needs more farmland to support it. Mali is facing severe environmental problems.

BURNING WOOD

Desertification and the loss of agricultural land are not caused only by drought. In Mali about 90 percent of energy needs are met by burning wood. Malians do not buy oil or natural gas to cook their food. They chop down trees and burn those. It is estimated that in Bamako, the capital city, 400,000 tons of wood are needed every year. Malians used to gather wood that had died naturally, but now that is not enough to meet the demand. Today, live trees are cut down, too. As the population increases, there is a need for more food, which means more livestock are being kept. The animals graze on the land, eating up the vegetation that helps to keep the soil in place. They also destroy the ability of the soil to

Malian girls carrying wood for cooking. The majority of energy used by Malians comes from wood.

recover just by trampling on it. All of this contributes to exposing the land to the wind. And there is plenty of wind in Mali. It blows southward from the Sahara, across the Sahel, and onto the exposed land. The exposed land dries up and is unable to support farming.

But Mali is fighting back. Working with the United Nations FAO (Food and Agriculture Organization), the country has become the center for the fight against desertification. It is a race to find solutions to the agricultural problems of the country while dealing with its enormous population growth. The program that has been put in place aims to improve the productivity of the soil and to train the farmers to make better use of the land.

THREATS TO THE NIGER RIVER

Unfortunately, the rapid growth of Mali's population spells trouble for the Niger River. As rain falls on the farmland, it picks up sediment and

A dust storm approaches a goat herd in the village of Kamaka in Mali.

Water hyacinth is a fast growing plant. If unchecked it can quickly cover bodies of water and starve aquatic life beneath from life-giving oxygen and sunlight.

washes it into the river channels. This slows the flow of water, and that interferes with the movement of the fish. Dams needed to control the flow of water also affect the environment. They change the nature of the river, often decreasing the flow of water to the habitats of the fish and wildlife around it. One of the greatest threats to rivers and lakes in Africa is a beautiful, but deadly weed called the water hyacinth. Like weeds everywhere it seems to thrive even when conditions are poor. It can choke an entire water system. All the nations in the region must put their resources together to try to control it from spreading further.

NATIONAL PARKS

There is very little wildlife in Mali and few national parks to visit. The main park and the largest game reserve in Mali is Parc National de la Boucle du Baoulé (Baoulé Bend National Park). It is located northwest of Bamako, in the western part of the country. Much of the wildlife that once lived there is gone. It is believed that hunting wiped out the populations of elephants, giraffes, buffalo, chimpanzees, and even lions that once roamed there. Today, monkeys are the animals visitors are most likely to see.

There are other, far more remote national parks. They are Parc National du Bafing, in the southwest, near the border with Guinea, and Réserve d'Ansongo-Menaka in the southeast, near the Niger border. The Réserve de Douentza is the most interesting in terms of wildlife. Located in the dry area between Mopti and Gao, it has a population of desert elephants. They move around as the seasons change, seeking food.

MINING AND THE ENVIRONMENT

What happens to a mine when there is no more gold to be found? The huge pit that has been dug is an enormous environmental hazard. Some companies have pledged to fill in these pits and return the land to the way it was. Time will tell whether this happens in Mali. The land there is already so fragile. It is possible that it will never again be useful for grazing or growing crops. Cyanide is used to separate the gold from the ore. This poison may remain in the soil for generations.

CYANIDE

Cyanide is a powerful chemical used to extract gold from rock. It is mixed with water to create a solution. This solution is then poured into large tanks that contain the gold-bearing rock. The rock and the cyanide mix together, and the gold is released from the rock. All the rock is then dumped at the mine site, with the cyanide still mixed in it. Over the years dust from these dumps blows over the nearby land, where it is breathed by the people living and farming in the region. The people breathing in the dust lose their ability to breathe as the passages in their lungs become closed. This can lead to death.

MALIANS

WHERE DO THE PEOPLE OF Mali come from? The earliest evidence of a humanlike creature in the region, known as Homo erectus, comes from tools dating as far back as 200,000 B.C. More modern human beings were likely living in northern Mali by about 50,000 B.C. Scientists believe that agriculture began in the region now known as the Sahara about 6,000 to 10,000 years ago, when the Sahara had a moister climate.

By about 1500 B.C. farming villages had developed along the Niger River. One of the first concentrations of people in a city in Mali was at Djenné, around 300 B.C. By about 500 A.D. towns and villages could be found throughout the region. There was a trend toward more militant people dominating and then absorbing other cultures over hundreds of years.

Mali has a very diverse population made up of eight main ethnic groups. Three-quarters of the population live in villages, towns, or cities. One-quarter of the population is nomadic. These people do not have permanent homes. Instead of living in villages, they live in family groups in temporary shelters that are easy to move when they look for new grazing land or water. Mali's ethnic groups live in fairly well defined areas, with very little overlap. However, as people are forced to leave their homelands and move into cities because of drought, the groups are becoming more mixed.

In spite of very difficult living conditions, Mali is a country of gracious, friendly, and hospitable people who share what little they have with strangers.

Above: **A Malian mother and her child.**

Opposite: **Girls in Bamako dressed in new clothes in celebration of Tabaski.**

In Mali people are born into different castes. A caste is a social class that determines a person's position in his or her culture. The top caste is the noble caste, while blacksmiths occupy the lowest caste. This caste system was firmly in place before the French colonized Mali. The system is not related to ethnic background. Most ethnic groups in Mali divided people into three major categories. There were the free people, also known as nobles. There was the professional group, such as people who worked with their hands. The lowest category included slaves. Only within Mali's modern history has it become possible for someone to practice a profession that once belonged to a higher caste.

THE MANDINKA

The Mandinka group makes up about half of Mali's total population and is believed to have originated about 4,000 years ago. Within that group are three ethnic subgroups. The largest is the Bambara, also known as the Bamana, who make up about 30 percent of the total population. They speak the Bamana or Bambara language.

A Bambara woman.

They are farmers as well as craftspeople and live in the southern part of the country, around Ségou and Bamako. The Bambara are famous for their masks and for their use of puppets in elaborate masquerades. The puppets are enormous, and the puppeteers actually hide inside so they can work them without being seen. This makes them seem very real and mysterious. Some puppets take the shape of mythical animals, while others look more like human figures. Songs accompany the puppets as

they dance and move around the villagers. Sometimes people who are watching join in and dance with a puppet. The puppets represent human emotions and human qualities, both good and evil. These characters are well known to the Bambara people.

The Malinke people also live around Bamako. Originally they were famed as hunters and gatherers. The Sarakole people, also known as the Soninke, live in the northwestern part of the country. They are known to be good traders and craftspeople. The Songhai are an ancient people who live mainly in northern Mali, between Timbuktu and Gao. They migrated into Mali around the 8th century A.D., according to one story. Most believe they are of Nilo-Saharan stock.

THE BOZO

The Bozo people are fishers who live in the central Niger River Delta and all along the river near Djenné and Lake Débo. Time seems to have stood still for the fisherman casting his net on the Niger River even though there are high-rise buildings in the background. Fishers have been working this way for centuries. The Niger River and its tributaries have an amazingly rich variety of species. People who have studied the river found nearly 250 species of freshwater fish, including 20 that are not found anywhere else in the world. Among the fish found in the Niger is the huge Nile perch, also known as the capitaine, as well as the tasty sunfish. The fish caught by the Bozo are one of the most important exports from Mali. The Bozo make their homes from sun-dried bricks.

THE PEUL

The Peul, also spelled Peulh, are also known as Fulani. They are a cattle-raising, nomadic people. They move around their territory in search of grazing land and water for their livestock. As they follow their livestock, they live in small, round, grass huts. They value their cattle more highly than their own lives. Most of the Peul are found within 100 miles (160 km) of the city of Mopti. It is estimated that there are between 850,000 and 1 million Fulani people in Mali.

A Fulani woman wearing large gold earrings. Gold is an indicator of wealth to the Fulani.

The Fulani have high standards of beauty and put a lot of effort into their grooming. Upper lips of Fulani women are tattooed. The Fulani women are also known for their distinctive earrings. They are made of gold that has been pounded into very thin sheets. The gold sheets are then twisted into shape. The earrings can be enormous in size and are sometimes attached to a cloth headdress or supported with a strap across the top of the woman's head that allows the earrings to dangle at either side of the face. The Fulani are found throughout at least six desert nations of West Africa.

THE TUAREG

The Tuareg are a nomadic people who are very much at home in the Sahara. They are known as the blue men of the Sahara because the blue color used to dye their robes often comes off on their skin. They are descended from the Berber people of North Africa and have similar Caucasoid features. In Tuareg culture men cover their faces. It is not proper for a Tuareg man to show his mouth, even when he is eating. Tuareg women, on the other hand, do not cover their faces. During the 1970s many Tuareg were forced to give up their way of life in the desert because they could not find food for their camels. When conditions improved, they were unable to return to their traditional way of life because they did not have money to buy camels. They are now sometimes seen in Timbuktu, sitting in cafés. One encounters them in the desert unexpectedly. They seem to appear out of nowhere, moving smoothly across the desert sand on their camels.

A Tuareg tribesman. The Tuareg are a tough people, able to survive in the harsh desert conditions.

To the outside world they are one of the enduring symbols of Africa and of the Sahara. They are at home in the desert, making use of oases where they can find water. Though there are no roads across the desert,

A group of Tuareg setting up camp in the desert. Tuareg claim that the desert is an intrinsic part of their lives and they cannot be separated from it.

there are tracks, called piste in French. The Tuareg know the desert well. It is their backyard and has great meaning and variety to them.

The Tuareg have had a very difficult history. Their nomadic way of life gave them a sense of freedom, and they resisted being assigned to a particular country. The boundaries drawn by the French around 1898, during the colonial period, broke up the Tuareg clans by relegating them to different nations. The process of desertification has added to their problems because it has made previously marginal lands unusable. But one of the biggest disruptions to traditional Tuareg life were the droughts that caused them to give up their camels and livestock. Drifting toward the towns, they lost their connection with the desert. Once that was broken, even after the rains returned, many were not able to return to their traditional way of life. It takes money to build up a herd of cattle and enough camels to maintain life in the desert. The Tuareg say, "We cannot be separated from the desert. It is there that we are free in every situation."

THE DOGON

The Dogon people, numbering about 500,000, live in an extremely dry and remote part of Mali called the Bandiagara Escarpment. The escarpment has been named a World Heritage Site by UNESCO, which brought it under international protection. Their territory is usually referred to as Dogon Country because it is separate from the rest of the nation. It is separate because of its physical location and also because the Dogon people have a unique culture and traditions that are centuries old and have resisted change. The Dogon rituals are not well known, in part because they have been protected so well. It is estimated that there are 700 Dogon villages and many Dogon dialects. The Dogon earn their living by growing onions on terraced farm plots.

DOGON CIRCUMCISION

As part of their religious beliefs the Dogon circumcise boys when they are 12 or 13 years old. This takes place in a very secret place called the circumcision grotto. In the Dogon village of Sangha the grotto, which is

LEAVING DOGON COUNTRY

What is it like for a person who was raised in one of the most remote areas of Mali to leave and arrive in the big capital city of Bamako? Assou Sagara, a Dogon who is now a guide, went to school in a Dogon village and then attended a French high school. When he went to Bamako for the first time, he said, "It was exceptional, different from everything I had seen in the past. It was very exciting and very big." Sagara's father was a soldier in France during World War II. "I had heard many things about the outside world from him." Most children growing up in the rural areas never leave their village.

similar to a cave, is painted with red and white figures, symbolizing animals and plants. These are used to educate the boys about Dogon traditions and folklore. The boys are kept in the grotto for 29 days. During this time their wounds heal. Herbs are used to help in this. This is also the time when they learn Dogon ways. The circumcision ceremony takes place every three years, but the exact date is decided by the head of the Dogon clan.

A special calabash made from a gourd is used in the ceremony. This is an extremely important and sacred object that holds a great deal of power for the Dogon. For this reason it must never be seen or held by a woman, especially a woman who is pregnant. It is believed that a pregnant woman who touches the calabash will lose the baby she is carrying.

The circumcision ceremony is considered to be the end of the boys' youth. They are now initiated into adult Dogon life. After they are circumcised, they receive presents.

DAMA CEREMONY

One of the most important Dogon rituals is the Dama ceremony. This takes place only once every 12 years and honors those who have died during that period. If the person who died was very important in the village, the ceremony will be longer and more impressive. The beginning of the ceremony invokes the making of masks. Then, over a number of days, the masked dancers descend from the top of the cliffs. Their dancing is dynamic and dramatic, and their costumes are brilliant and colorful. Cowry shells, once used as currency in West Africa, are sewn onto leather. Cowry shells are still highly prized because they represent something that is so very far away—the ocean. For some ceremonies the wood masks can be attached to headpieces that rise two stories above the dancer. This is the *sirige* mask. They are so well made, however, that the dancer can whip his head around, displaying the headpiece.

During these ceremonies the masks are said to have been danced, and the ceremony is not complete until this has taken place. The Dogon

Left: **The Dogon performing a funerary dance with the masks that are meant to instill fear and awe.**

Opposite: **Traditional Dogon painting on a rock wall near the Bandiagara cliffs. These are used to educate the Dogon boys about Dogon culture and beliefs.**

The Dogon believe that the masks that they wear contain the spirits of their deceased.

put great stress on this. Otherwise, evil things can happen to the people. Their crops might fail or the village women might suffer miscarriages. Women specifically must stay away from the masks. They may view the ceremony from a distance, along with the children, but they do not take part. Children are too young to understand the true meaning of the masks and the ceremony. They will be taught about them when they are older. In some Dogon dances men wear costumes that include bras, indicating they are taking the part of the women.

Their costumes are striking and sometimes frightening, which is what the wearers intend. The masks are meant to frighten because it is believed that they contain the souls of the dead ancestors. The ancestors can protect the Dogon from evil spirits, but they must be honored. Because the masks are so powerful, they are made in great

secrecy. Women are not allowed to see the masks being made. Women give birth to children and so are believed to have great power. It would be dangerous if such powerful people were present when the masks were being made.

In addition to their close connections to their ancestors, the Dogon believe they can predict the future. In every Dogon village there is an elder known as a griot. He tells the story of the Dogon people over and over again, teaching the younger generation its own history. This is called oral history. When people do not have books, they learn their history from their elders. Griots can recite the history of their people going back through many generations. They are precious resources in their communities.

To look into the future, the griot takes a stick and draws a grid in the sand. He does this in the evening and then places morsels of food on the grid. That evening the food attracts desert jackals that leave their paw prints on the pattern. The next morning the griot and other elders gather to read the tracks left by the jackals, and from that, they predict the events that will occur.

LIFESTYLE

IN MALI MOST PEOPLE LIVE in rural areas. Daily life involves farming, preparing meals, and tending livestock. Most of the objects people need for their daily lives are made by the people themselves. Women make pottery and baskets and also weave cloth. Women and girls walk great distances to get water for cooking and washing. They must also gather wood to use for cooking fires. These tasks take up many hours of each day. Grain, such as millet, must be pounded into flour, another chore that takes time. Women also do most of the farming. There is very little leisure time for a woman living in the countryside. Men and boys usually look after the livestock. This usually means walking great distances to take them to an area to eat and drink. Men also gather construction materials to build houses.

Above: **A girl living in rural Mali washing cooking pots.**

Opposite: **Many Malians still travel by carts pulled by oxen.**

A NATION OF FARMERS

About 80 percent of Malians grow crops for food and raise livestock. Some of them earn a living by fishing. All of these agricultural activities depend on rainfall. The land is very fragile; the topsoil can be blown away by a strong windstorm. The bushes and trees that hold the land in place are also nibbled away by the goats that can be found almost everywhere. And Mali has about 6 million head of cattle that graze on plants for food.

When drought hits, as it does fairly often, all of these activities come to a halt. There is no vegetation for the cattle. There is no water for them or for the crops. The goats eat the last bits of roots in the ground, which allows topsoil to blow away. Even when the rains return, it is difficult for

After marriage, Malian women leave their own homes to live with their husbands' families.

the land to be used successfully for farming and grazing because the topsoil is gone.

In Bamako and the other cities people must have cash-earning jobs to survive. Many people, however, manage to grow vegetables on small plots of land, and some also keep chickens right in the city. This is likely to change, however, as more and more people crowd into Bamako seeking work. There will be less room for farming and keeping chickens. Buildings in the cities are often made with the same simple materials as those in the countryside. Mud or adobe constructions are common.

EXTENDED FAMILIES

In Mali, especially in the rural areas, people live in extended family groups. These usually center around the husband's family. A Muslim man may have as many as four wives. Each wife has her own house, where she lives with her young children. Her husband will stay with her on certain nights. Grown boys who are not yet married live in their own huts. When they marry, they bring their wives to the family compound, and each couple then has its own hut. Often the wives will cook together in a kitchen hut built just for that purpose. The elderly stay with their children until they die.

MARRIAGE

Marriage is at the heart of Malian life. Rituals and celebrations involve the whole family. The extended family, including aunts and uncles, who play a major role in their relatives' lives, take part. In Mali a young woman marries into her husband's family. Marriage ceremonies are elaborate, even though most people earn very little money. There are tremendous financial obligations, especially for the groom. His family must give presents, either gifts or money, to the bride's family. This is considered to be compensation to the bride's family because they are losing an important worker. For a young herder it will take about two years' labor to earn enough to make this payment. This certainly puts a strain on the couple, especially the woman, who now must fit into the new household and prove herself. The bride must now work in the fields belonging to her husband's family, so they gain a productive person.

There are three types of marriages in Mali. Traditional marriage is based on ethnic beliefs and rituals. Civil marriage is based on the laws of the nation. Religious marriage follows the laws of the couple's religion, usually Islam. It is possible to have more than one type of marriage. In the cities people often combine two or even three of these types of marriage. By going through more than one ceremony, a couple can keep its civil rights, such as pensions, but also the privileges of its family heritage. At the same time the couple honors the obligations of its religion.

A Malian family making their way to the market at Djenné.

Marriage takes place at an early age in Mali. In the countryside the average age at marriage is 16. By 19, half of all the women have had their first child. As many as 10 percent of women have their first child by the age of 15, an age when they could still be considered children

A young Fulani boy crossing the river with his herd of cattle.

themselves. The more children a woman has, the better her position in the household. Children are seen as helpers for the future. They provide labor for farming and cattle herding. It is not unusual for a man in Mali to have more than one wife at the same time. This is allowed in the Muslim religion, and it is also common among the Dogon, who are not Muslims. Having more than one wife creates very complicated and crowded households. A family group may consist of 60 people. When a man has more than one wife, his children occupy different positions in the home. The wives also maintain very close ties to their own parents and other relatives. Over time an intricate web of relationships is built up, because the children of a man's wives are related to each other as half siblings, and they are related to other wives in a quasiparental way. Children and wives compete for attention, favors, food, and money.

CROSSING OF THE CATTLE

In a nation where cattle are so important, it is not surprising that there is a ceremony devoted to them. Each year Fulani boys drive their cattle to grazing lands far from home to save them from the annual floods. They are away for a whole year, and when they return, they come back as young men, ready to take wives and their place in Fulani society. Their return in December is the occasion for a great celebration called the Deegal. At this time the cattle cross the Niger River at several places, including the village of Diafarabé, arriving back into the area of Mopti.

On that first day unmarried men and women dress up to take part in the Promenade des Jeunes (Parade of the Youth). People also decorate their houses for the occasion, painting the doors with white clay and the floors with dark clay. Girls buy special mats for their boyfriends to sit on. They will talk all through the night. All the people celebrate by eating, drinking, and dancing well into the night. The crossing of the cattle ceremony has been taking place since 1818, when the village of Diafarabé was founded. It is a coming of age celebration for young Fulani men.

DOGON

The Dogon people have one of the richest cultures in all of Africa. They have a belief system that encompasses the entire universe. The Dogon are animists, which means they believe in a great number of spirits that affect humans by either helping or harming them. The Dogon reenact the creation of the world through their ceremonial dances. Most of their dances are known as funerary because they are dedicated to their ancestors. The Dogon feel a very close connection to their ancestors and in particular to the souls of the dead members of their community. The Dogon wrap their dead in bark taken from the baobab tree. Once every three years they cut the bark from one of the baobab trees in their village. Then they allow the tree to rest and regrow the bark before they cut it again. During this period they place a bandage on the tree to aid in the healing. It protects the exposed portion where the bark was removed.

The bark of the baobab tree is used to wrap Dogon who have passed on. The baobab tree is then wrapped to aid its healing.

The Dogon revere their dead and bury them in niches that have been built into vertical cliff faces like this.

About 1,000 years ago Islam was making its way into Mali, brought by the Arab traders coming in from North Africa. The Dogon were committed to their animist beliefs and knew they would have to move far away in order to maintain their own faith. They fled to the Bandiagara escarpment. That area is extremely isolated and very difficult to reach, helping the Dogon maintain their traditions and beliefs. Their villages are built on vertical cliff faces, making them safe from outsiders. Not only do they build their houses there, they also build their granaries, the buildings where they store grains. Most important to the Dogon are the niches in the cliffs where they bury their dead. For all the time that the Dogon have lived there, they have kept their dead very close. This connects them on a daily basis with their ancestors.

EDUCATION

Mali has an extremely rich history of educational pursuits. The best example of this is the manuscripts of Timbuktu. They nearly disappeared because of neglect. The great wealth of books and manuscripts in Timbuktu came to the world's attention in 1967. Recognizing the need to preserve the materials, UNESCO provided money for a manuscript conservation center in Timbuktu. But the project was enormous, and very little was accomplished over the next thirty years. Through the centuries many of the books were kept in caves by families in Timbuktu. Although this kept them out of the harsh heat, it did not protect them from termites and high humidity during the rainy season. In time the materials began to deteriorate. It was crucial to find a way to preserve them to make them available for future generations.

HARVARD UNIVERSITY HELPS OUT

When Henry Louis Gates Jr., the chairman of Harvard University's African and African-American Studies Department, went to Timbuktu in 1997 to learn about the documents he started a process to preserve the documents and make them available to more people. "I opened the doors to the books and manuscripts piled up in a dusty room by the thousands, and Professor Gates broke down in tears," said Abdel Kader Haidara, director of his family's library in Timbuktu. Gates suddenly had proof that Africa had a written heritage, something he had been told did not exist. Gates was instrumental in getting funding from the Andrew W. Mellon Foundation to start to restore material from the extensive Haidara family library.

SCANNING THE MANUSCRIPTS

Now the Library of Congress has embarked on a project to scan the manuscripts and make them available on the Internet. This will spread the information in them all over the world, giving scholars access to materials that previously were known only to a few people. In addition,

Haidara has been working with the Ahmad Baba Center in Timbuktu to collect and preserve manuscripts from many families and make them available to scholars.

In 2006 a small collection of manuscripts from the Mamma Haidara Collection, from Haidara's family, toured the United States. It was first shown at the International Museum of Muslim Cultures in Jackson, Mississippi.

EDUCATION TODAY

Although Mali is a country rich in culture and tradition, it is poor when it comes to education and literacy. It is considered one of the least developed countries in the world. In order to develop, a nation must have citizens who can read. In Mali only about one-third of children attend primary schools. The problem is especially severe in the rural areas, although there are efforts to improve the situation. Boys outnumber girls in schools by a huge margin. Among adults it is estimated that only about 20 percent of the people can read, and again, men outnumber women in this category. This means they cannot read instructions or work in any kind of job that requires them to read. It also means they cannot follow written instructions for taking medication.

ORAL TRADITION

Mali has an oral tradition. Information is passed along from parent to child, from elders to the rest of the group, in conversation. The history of the Dogon people, for example, is told by the griot, who himself learned it from an older griot. A griot (GREE-oh) is a storyteller, musician, historian, and seer, someone who interprets signs and omens and foretells the future for his people.

Although there is a law that says primary education is free and required, there are not enough schools for all the children in Mali to attend. Another reason many people are not educated is that children in rural areas are likely to become farmers like their parents. If they are in school, they cannot work in the fields. Girls are also married at a very young age in Mali. Even before they marry, however, their parents require them to work at home or to work for others as maids, to earn money. Girls must help out with cooking and cleaning because their mothers are usually busy taking care of the younger children. With an average of seven children born to each woman, there is a lot of work to do. Rural parents do not see any practical benefit in educating girls.

Tourists taking a look at early manuscripts found in Timbuktu. These manuscripts are evidence of the existence of early written African script where there was previously thought to be none.

Another issue with education is the level of teacher training. In many cases teachers have only a ninth-grade education and are not trained to be teachers. They are basically reentering the classroom they just left as students and are expected to pass along whatever they learned. There is very little to hold the students' interest. Because of the difficulty of reaching people in the remote, rural areas, the United States Agency for International Development (USAID) began a teacher-training program through a radio network. It reaches 85 percent of Mali's teachers and has helped improve the passing rate among sixth-grade children to 70 percent.

IMPROVING EDUCATION

Organizations including USAID and Oxfam (an organization founded in Oxford, England, dedicated to famine relief) are working in Mali to

Even though basic education is compulsory in Mali, many children still do not attend school as they are needed by their families to farm.

improve the level of education and the number of children attending schools. In the rural areas USAID built 1,740 community schools over a seven-year period from 1995 to 2003. The enrollment in school in that area nearly doubled. At the same time the program tried to improve the training of teachers and to distribute books in Mali's different languages. Many schools cannot afford to buy books without outside help. Although they distributed more than 30,000 books, that is just a tiny number when compared with the number of students who need them. Many children drop out of school because the books they do have do not relate to their lives at all. The program of studies is often still based on the French model, which has almost nothing to do with life in Mali today. The role of the Mali government in improving education is to accept all the aid offered to it. According to Robert Pringle, former U.S. Ambassador to Mali (1987–1990), "The Malians have become expert to sustaining aid flows from multiple sources. . . . Mali is now the largest per capita recipient of foreign aid in the region."

A scrubland school in Dogon county. Thanks to a program put in place by USAID, more rural children now have access to an education.

Oxfam's program works to combat the dropout rate among girls by using a very different approach. They employ women from the same communities to visit schools and talk about their own personal success. This is called the animatrice model and uses non-professional teachers. The use of local women is thought to be the best approach, since they have experienced life in those communities and understand the obstacles facing girls. Some of the areas they have targeted with this program are among the most difficult to reach in Mali—the nomadic and seminomadic people of the north, including the Tuareg.

ADULT LITERACY

One of the most positive results of the improvement in children's education is the desire of adults to learn to read. Since they must work during the day, they meet at night in classrooms that do not have electricity. An ingenious battery-powered projector has been developed just for use in these dark classrooms. It is called *kinkajou*, the name of a nocturnal

Distribution of these simple bed nets has helped to curb Malaria, a disease that is transmitted by mosquitoes.

animal with exceptional nighttime vision. Literacy lesson material is provided on microfilm so it can be used in the projector. USAID is funding this program. Many foreign-aid organizations and nongovernmental organizations are working in Mali in an effort to raise literacy standards throughout the population. These organizations know that with more education, the citizens will be better equipped to make good decisions about their lives. They can understand the choices offered to them, read about different ideas, and exercise free will. In a young democratic society such as Mali's, literacy is an important way to break free from autocratic rule.

HEALTH AND DISEASE

Health care in general is very limited in Mali. Most women give birth without any medical assistance at all. In the rural areas one of every five children dies before the age of 5. The average life expectancy for those who make it into adulthood is estimated at 47 years for men and 48 years for women.

Malaria, a disease that is carried by mosquitos, is one of the most prevalent in Africa. While malaria strikes people of all ages, children under the age of 5 are particularly affected by this disease, which is marked by a very high fever. More children under the age of 5 die from malaria than from any other cause. While medications to prevent malaria are extremely expensive, and not widely available, there is a simple, inexpensive way to keep people from being bitten by mosquitoes. Bed nets, also known as mosquito nets, are treated with insecticide and then draped all around the area where someone is sleeping. The USAID program that provides these nets without charge has been a great help in curbing this disease. It only costs USAID a few dollars for each net. The insecticide in them lasts for five years. More than 132,000 were distributed by USAID in 2004.

RIVER BLINDNESS

There are certain diseases that affect people in Africa that are hardly known in the rest of the world. For many years the most ordinary sight in Mali and other West African nations was that of a child holding onto a stick. At the other end of the stick was a blind old man. It was the child's job to lead that man around because the man had lost

A victim of river blindness being led through his village.

his sight. People who live along a river, such as the people in Mali, are exposed to a disease called *onchocerciasis*, which is commonly known as river blindness. It is a disease caused by a black fly. The flies breed in water that carries the disease and then spread it to the people through tiny worms. Once the disease begins there is no way to stop it. In some villages people had abandoned their homes near the river because there was no way to avoid contracting the disease. In others every adult had become blind from the disease. Among its symptoms is skin that has become scaly and itchy. In Africa in the 1980s it was estimated that 20 million people were infected. It was almost impossible to avoid the infection because river water was needed for every aspect of daily life, including bathing, drinking, fishing, and washing clothes.

Then in 1987 a remarkable medical plan was put into effect. Merck & Co., an American pharmaceutical firm, had discovered a drug called Mectizan that could prevent river blindness. Even more amazing, the company decided that it would donate the medicine to every person who lived in an area that was affected by the disease. The company worked with a number of private and public groups, including the World Health Organization, the World Bank, the United Nations Children's Fund, and Sight Savers International to bring the drug to every village that needed it for as long as it was needed. Merck's executives knew it was the only way to distribute a medication to people who had no way of reaching a health clinic. Even the tiny cost of the drug, about $3 a person, was completely out of reach in this extremely poor nation. The drug must be taken just once a year for a period of 20 years to give a person lifelong protection.

Merck and Company was the pharmaceutical firm that discovered a drug that could prevent river blindness.

The result has been phenomenal. More than 1 billion doses of the medicine have been distributed. River blindness has been virtually wiped out in Africa. Forty-five million people have been treated and now face bright futures. Instead of sitting under trees, unable to work, they can do their farming and fishing and support themselves and their families. Only people who do not have the disease already can be treated. The drug only prevents the disease; it does not cure it.

RELIGION

ISLAM IS THE DOMINANT RELIGION in Mali today. People who follow Islam are called Muslims. Muslim practices vary enormously throughout the Islamic world. Most Muslims in Mali are followers of the Sunni branch of Islam. In Mali it is estimated that 80 percent of the population is Muslim. A tiny number of people, from 2 to 4 percent of the population, are Christian. Half of them are Catholic, the other half Protestant. The remainder, close to 20 percent, follows traditional religious practices, also known as animism.

ISLAM

The type of Islam followed in Mali is considered among the most tolerant in the world. Women do not cover their faces, and civil law, not religious law, governs the way people live. Malians usually combine their devotion to Islam with their traditional religious practices, taking those parts that suit their African way of life. This makes it easier for people from other religious groups to travel, work, and live in Mali. Many Malians do not see a conflict between proclaiming their faith in Allah, the Muslim name for God, and also believing in their traditional religion.

Islam has had a long history in Mali, dating back to the 8th century A.D., when traders began to introduce the religion as they traveled southward across the Sahara. In the beginning the practice of the religion was confined to educated people—rulers, merchants, and religious leaders themselves. The rural people mainly followed their traditional religion.

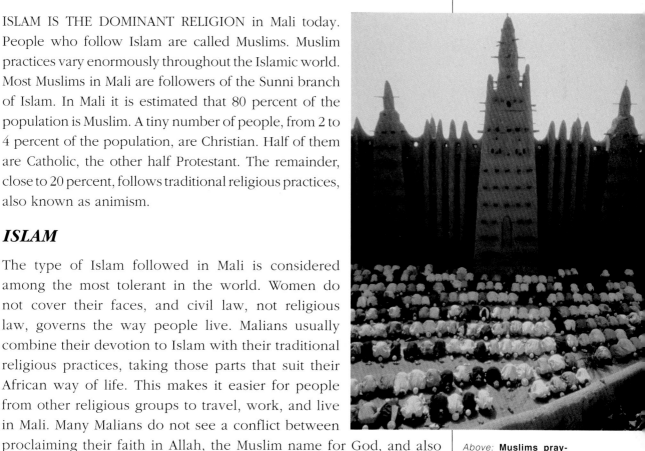

Above: **Muslims praying in front of the Great Mosque.**

Opposite: **Muslims gather for prayers at the end of Ramadan.**

97

A man reading the Koran. Most Malians closely adhere to the teachings of the Koran.

The practice of Islam grew during the French colonial period because the French administrators used religious leaders to help them control people living in rural areas.

Although most of the people in Mali are considered Muslims, the country is not ruled as a theocracy, which is a country where religious law comes before civil law. It is a thoroughly democratic country, following the rule of law set out in its constitution.

The Islamic calendar is based on the movement of the moon, so its 12 months add up to 354 days. However, it takes 365.25 days for the earth to circle the sun. As a result Islamic religious celebrations do not have fixed dates, as New Year's Day or Christmas Day do. Instead, they vary from year to year, occurring in different seasons. Each month in the Islamic calendar begins when the new moon, the crescent moon, can be seen in the night sky. The Islamic calendar began in the year 622 A.D.

FIVE PILLARS OF ISLAM

There are five elements of the Islamic religion that guide everyday life. They are the testimony of faith, prayer, giving support to the needy, fasting during the month of Ramadan, and making a pilgrimage to Mecca for anyone who is able.

The testimony of faith means that the person must say, "There is no true god but Allah, and Muhammad is His prophet." This declaration is considered the most important pillar of Islam.

Muslims pray five times every day, kneeling and facing the direction of Mecca, a city in Saudi Arabia that was the birthplace of Muhammad. These prayers are performed at dawn, noon, midafternoon, sunset, and night. People are allowed to pray almost anywhere, including at work, at school, in a field, or anywhere in public. One does not have to go to a mosque to pray.

The pilgrimage is a sacred duty, but it is required only of a person who can afford the trip and is healthy enough to make the journey. This pilgrimage, called a hajj, is performed in the twelfth month of the Islamic calendar.

A display of carvings and masks used by believers of animism.

Observing Ramadan is an important part of practicing Islam. This is a monthlong period in which Muslims fast from sunrise to sunset to honor the moment when their sacred book, the Koran, was revealed to the prophet Muhammad. Muslims may not eat or drink anything at all during the day, every day, for the month. In some years Ramadan is celebrated in the summer; in some years it is in the fall, according to the 354-day lunar calendar.

ANIMISM

Before the coming of Islam, most Malians were animists. Animism is a belief that spirits exist in natural objects. That means every object is sacred and must be respected. This puts believers totally in touch with their environment. They respect every animal and object, such as trees or rocks because they believe everything and everyone has a soul. Today, many Malians continue to hold this belief while also practicing Islam or Christianity.

LANGUAGE

MALI IS A COUNTRY THAT HAS MANY languages. Bambara is used widely in West Africa, especially in business and trade. It is very similar to Dioula, a language spoken throughout the region. This means a Bambara speaker can communicate with people in a very wide region of West Africa. Malinke is spoken in the area around the borders with Senegal and Guinea. Senoufo is used in other parts of Mali as well as in parts of Burkina Faso and Cote d'Ivoire.

Dialects are variations of a language. They often develop in isolated areas where there is little contact with other people. In the Bandiagara Escarpment, where the Dogon people live, there are nearly fifty major dialects. Sanga is one of the most important of those languages. Dogon languages vary so widely that some Dogon people cannot understand the language spoken by other Dogon. In this case language acts to separate people. People often develop specific words for tools, for example, that are important in their daily lives.

The official language of Mali is French, but it is not the language spoken by most Malians. French is spoken by people with a higher education, and it is the language spoken by the administration, the people in government.

BAMBARA

The language spoken by most people in Mali is Bambara. It is estimated that 80 percent of the people in Mali speak Bambara even though the Bambara people make up only 35 percent of the population. The Bambara, however, live in the more urban areas of Mali, especially in Bamako, so they have had more opportunity to spread their language. During the colonial period Bambara was used by the African soldiers in the French colonial army, so other Malians picked it up. Because the newspapers and television and radio

Opposite: **A boy learning to read at a Madrasa, or religious school.**

BIENVENUE CHEZ KENEKO DARA
AU CAMPEMENT DE "L'AMITIE
BAR_RESTAU DOGON"
CHAMBRES Objets. D'ard   BOISSONS.FRAICHE
◄ 3M   A.KOUNDOU
              GUINEL

Two boys showing a directional sign at the Dogon village of Koundou.

programs that developed after independence were centered in Bamako, where the majority of people are Bambara speakers, the language spread even more widely and rapidly. There is even an organization dedicated to spreading Bambara throughout the nation. This organization, Direction Natinale de l' Alphabétisation Fonctionelle et de la Linguistique Appliquée (DNAFLA), was created in 1975. It also promotes the use of other Malian languages, including Fulfuldé, Songhai, Senoufo, Dogon, Soninke, and Tamashek.

For all these reasons many people in Mali speak several languages. Many speak several tribal languages as well as French. English is gaining inroads, too, especially in Bamako. Dogon is spreading widely as the Dogon gain access to education. They are a smart and energetic people who have more influence than their small population size would suggest.

SAYING HELLO

In hurried western life, with everyone rushing around all the time, people pay little attention to the way they greet people. Giving a quick "Hello, how are you," without waiting for an answer is normal. But in Africa people take time to greet each other and even go through an elaborate ritual that shows they really care about each other. Among the Dogon, for example, the ritual remains an important part of the culture. It begins as two people approach each other. Long before they are actually standing close together, they call out questions about the person's health and then about his or her family, parents, and even animals. Each question is answered. The other person goes through the same questions, and they are answered as well. All the while, they have been walking closer together and then even passing each other, but they keep up the exchange. It is a ritual, and the answers may be ritualistic, but the people do acknowledge each other in a very important way. It is particularly important to bring up the spouse and children and then the parents in the greeting to show the importance of one's relatives.

SPEAKING BAMBARA

Bambara is widely spoken in Mali. Here are some useful and common words.

Welcome	*i ni chè*	Food:	
Yes	*owó*	Fish	*jègè*
No	*ayi*	Sugar	*sukara*
Thank you	*i ni cé*	Rice	*malo* (uncooked) *kini* (cooked)
		Banana	*namasa*
Numbers:		Bread	*buru*
One	*kelen*	Milk	*nono*
Two	*fila*	Water	*ji*
Three	*saba*		
Four	*naani*		
Five	*duuro*		

ARTS

ART IS AN EXPRESSION OF culture. Mali is particularly rich in cultures that express themselves through music, architecture, crafts, and dance. Fragments of textiles found in caves on the Bandiagara Escarpment show that this art form was well established in the region by the 11th century.

In Mali, as in much of Africa, art is something to be used, not just admired. African art has power because it is made for a purpose, usually for use in a ceremony or a ritual. The objects made by people for their ceremonies gain power when they are used. Each ethnic group in Mali practices its unique expressions of art.

TUAREG CRAFTS

As a nomadic people the Tuareg carry everything they need on their camels. They have become expert leather craftspeople, using the skins from goats. Saddlebags, which hold all sorts of useful items, including clothing, household goods, and food, are beautifully made. Women work on the skins, which are carefully softened and tanned before the intricately detailed decoration work is begun. The Tuareg color bits of leather and then press these precise geometric shapes into the leather background. One of their techniques involves stitching that is used to create patterns on the leather. They add fringes of leather to the bottoms of leather panels. A woman will spend months working on one saddlebag, which is meant to last for years and years. It is placed across the camel, with a flat piece of leather connecting the two bags. The bags hang down on either side of the camel, within easy reach of the rider if he or she needs something. The same technique is used to make carrying cases for the Koran, the Muslim holy book, and for small purses worn on a long cord hanging around the neck.

Opposite: **Mali cloth on sale at a market at Djenné.**

Tuareg purses are particularly intriguing. The case is in two parts: the inner part is open at one end and holds the treasured items. The outer part is made to slide along the cord and cover the inner case completely, hiding the contents and making it impossible for a thief to take something out without the wearer noticing it. They are as beautiful as they are practical and are one of the most popular items visitors look to purchase when visiting Mali.

The Tuareg make their camel saddles from wood, leather, and bits of metal. Like the saddlebags, the saddle itself is decorated, colored, and embellished all over. The front and back of the saddle are very high to give support to the rider.

MALI CLOTH

Many ideas and material objects have come to us from Africa, often without our knowing their origin. Many of us may have worn the beautiful material known as Mali cloth or mud cloth without knowing where it came from. The Bambara name for mud cloth is *bògòlanfini* (bo-ho-lahn-FEE-nee), which means "mud cloth." The word *bogolan* comes

THE BAMBARA HEADRESS

The best-known symbols of the Bambara people are the headdresses that look like antelope heads, with great antlers that are carved from wood. These represent a legendary or mythical figure, Tyi Wara. The Bambara believe that they learned how to farm, and particularly how to plant maize (corn), from Tyi Wara. During the important planting and harvesting seasons, ceremonies are held in which the antelope headdresses are worn by dancers. The Bambara also craft masks using the antelope symbol for their initiation rites. These symbols are very powerful in the Bambara culture.

from a local tree. *Fini* means "cloth" in the Bambara language. Traditionally, the leaves from the *bogolon* tree are used in the dyeing process.

Bògòlanfini is a special craft of the Bambara people. It is made by an ancient technique that requires a great deal of handwork as well as artistic ability and knowledge of the Bambara culture. The cloth is usually coarse and is made from cotton that is locally grown, hand spun, and then worked on a hand loom. Traditionally, men have woven the cloth strips, usually about 4 inches wide and 72 inches in length. Once the strips are woven, they are sewn together to make a panel. This is usually about 32 to 45 inches wide, depending on the number of strips used.

Once the plain cloth panel has been completed, it is turned over to the women, who create the intricate patterns from dyes that are made of natural materials, including leaves and tree bark. These patterns and the techniques used to create them are a family affair. Mothers have passed the knowledge down to their daughters, generation after generation. The patterns are more than decorative. They are symbols that can be read to reveal Bambara history and beliefs. Some of the motifs are very specific, such as drums or houses, animals or towns. Some are more symbolic and are harder for an outsider to read. The artist repeats the symbols over and over, enclosing them within geometric shapes on the cloth. All the symbols taken together create their own pattern, and no two pieces of Mali cloth are exactly alike.

A woman painting a cotton rug at a *Bògòlanfini* workshop in Segou.

Traditionally, the cloth was worn only for special occasions, such as Bambara women's initiation ceremonies. Hunters were allowed to wear garments made of Mali cloth because it was believed the cloth was so powerful, it would protect them during the hunt.

Today, the tradition is being kept alive in special associations, including the Boutique des Femmes (women's shop) in Ségou. The association brings together women and girls who share their skills. The older women have the chance to pass along their knowledge to the girls, who learn a useful skill.

Another group, the Maison des Jeunes (youth club) in Bamako, offers workshops in *bògòlan*. This club is designed to offer young people a place to gather and learn a skill, rather than just hanging around the streets of the capital. With these skills, they can earn money by selling the crafts they have made.

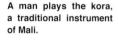

A man plays the kora, a traditional instrument of Mali.

MUSIC

Thanks to its different ethnic groups and their own unique histories, Mali has a rich musical tradition. The best-known musical instrument is the *djembe* drum. The name is also spelled *jembe*. The *djembe* drum is made of wood with goatskin stretched over the top to form the drumming surface. Leather cords are used to secure the goatskin and are often laced in an attractive geometric pattern.

Oumou Sangaré sings about situations that many Malians, especially women, are familiar with.

The *djembe* drum is usually held between the legs, with the drummer sitting down. It allows the drummer to bring out a rich variety of tones and is often used by storytellers. It also provides rhythms for dancers. The sound travels very well, which makes it useful for sending messages between villages. The villagers can interpret the messages from the rhythms that were played.

The *kora* is the most widely used traditional stringed instrument in Mali. Griots, also called *jalis*, use the *kora* to tell their stories, perhaps because it is so versatile in the sounds it makes. With its 21 strings stretched over a long neck, the *kora* is a very complicated instrument to play. The strings are plucked with the fingers. The *kora* is played at important ceremonies, such as weddings and naming days, when infants are given their names.

The best-known female traditional Malian singer is Oumou Sangaré, nicknamed "The songbird of Wassoulou," her ancestral home. In her music she tells the story of Mali, especially the problems that Malian women face. She sings about traditions that can make life very difficult for women, such as arranged marriages, and about the hard work women must do. Much of this material comes from her own upbringing. She saw how much her mother struggled in her own household. She conveys this in an unusually heartfelt manner, reaching out to the listener in a very direct way, especially younger people who feel she understands modern problems better than many traditional male singers. She is a communicator as much as she is a musician.

ALI FARKA TOURÉ

Ali Farka Touré is a popular musican from Mali who is known for being able to fuse elements of both Western and African music.

The unique sound of Ali Farka Touré combines the modern acoustic guitar with African ideas and a style that is close to American blues. When he first heard African-American performers, Farka Touré realized that American music was deeply tied to its African roots. He was inspired by this music, and it found its way into his own sound. His music has been described as "sinuous," which means it winds around and around, drawing the listener closer. He was born near Timbuktu in 1939 into a northern Mali family that traced its roots back many generations and was considered to be noble. He began playing a simple one-string African guitar called the *gurkel* as a boy. Later in his life he took up the acoustic guitar and adapted its sound to suit his artistic needs. He combined his life as a musician with a traditional Malian life as a farmer. Even when he became very well known, he continued to live in a village. One of his best-known albums is *Talking Timbuktu*. Farka Touré always dressed in traditional clothing, which contrasted with his very modern guitar. That combination shows that he was able to combine these two different worlds in his music. In spite of his worldwide success as a musician, Farka Touré always thought of himself as a farmer first and often left his musical career behind to tend to his farm. His village and his family meant everything to him. He died on March 7, 2006, after a long struggle with bone cancer. In many ways he symbolized Mali and its music to a worldwide audience.

TINARIWEN

Tinariwen is a musical group that is considered the voice of the Kel Tamasgheq people, also known as the Tuareg. It was formed in 1982 and led by Ibrahim Ag Alhabib. The recent history of the Tuareg people, their suffering during the resistance to both French rule and the Mali army, is told through their music. Tinariwen has been an important part of the Festival in the Desert.

Traditional Tuareg music utilizes the shepherd flute, the *imzad* fiddle, and the *tinde* drum. But the threats to Tuareg culture inspired the musicians to give up these instruments and use the electric guitar, electric bass, and drums. These modern instruments were a revolt against everything they knew from their past. They still use their music to tell the story of the Tuareg very much the way the Dogon griots use music and storytelling to relate the history of the Dogon people. Protest songs are at the heart and soul of Tinariwen's lyrics.

CONNECTING CULTURES

In 2006 Tinariwen performed *Songs of the Desert* at a remarkable concert in New York City's Symphony Space Theater. When the concert began, all the singers wore traditional *tagilmusts*, headdresses made of cloth that protect the wearer from wind and sun, entirely covering their faces except for their eyes. These wraps loosened a bit during the first half of the program. The New York audience followed every song with enthusiasm, and it was clear that though they could not understand the words Tinariwen sang, they understood their spirit. In the second half of the program the *tagilmusts* began to unwind more and more, and by the end of the program, one of the performers had taken his off entirely. This was a tremendous sign of acceptance. He felt at home on this stage in this big city as he sang about his homeland, 10,000 miles away.

GOLDSMITHS OF BAMAKO

In ancient times the goldsmiths of Bamako were well known. Since Mali had a ready source of gold, the smiths learned to make beautiful objects from the precious metal. In recent years the gold market at Bamako has become a favorite place for visitors. At the Bamako Jewelry School the master goldsmith Gaoussou Dembele teaches the art of goldsmithing. Mali gold jewelry reflects the nation's cultures and takes its inspiration from mythology as well as from plants and animals. Gold is a very soft metal that can be worked by hand. Goldsmithing techniques are very ancient and do not require modern equipment or even electricity. The metal can be engraved, hammered, or flattened using simple tools. The goldsmith can heat

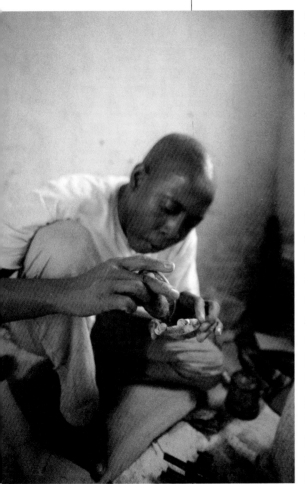

A goldsmith concentrates on crafting a piece of gold into a work of art using only simple tools.

the metal using a bellow made of goatskin. Because gold has been mined in Mali for so long, the goldsmiths have a lot of experience in working with the metal and in creating beautiful jewelry that reflects the cultures of Mali.

PICASSO AND AFRICAN ART

The great artist Pablo Picasso was tremendously influenced by the African objects he saw. In Africa art is not something separate from the usefulness of an object. This is true, for example, of the Dogon masks, which are made for specific ceremonies. Picasso more than any other artist understood and felt the power and meaning these works had for the people who made and used them. He said that he "contracted the virus of African art" in 1907 when he visited the ethnographic museum in Paris and saw African masks there. He said he feared the power of the masks he saw and felt an intensely strong connection with the work. They made such a strong impression on him that he immediately interpreted them in his own work, starting with his painting *Les Demoiselles d'Avignon* (*Women of Avignon*). He understood that the African artists exaggerated some features to emphasize the power of those features. This is why some masks have extremely large eyes or enormous mouths. That was done to communicate information to the person seeing the mask. The influence of the animal masks from Mali can actually be seen in his paintings. Many art critics believe that when Picasso came into contact with African works, it changed the entire direction of art.

DOGON ARCHITECTURE

The Dogon make everything they use in their daily lives, including their houses and the granaries that hold their supplies of grain. The granaries are built on stilts to protect the maize and millet from insects. Each granary has a small opening cut into the wall. This opening is closed with a carved wood door. Often the carving depicts figures of ancestors. The door latch is very well made. A piece of wood fitted out with pins that form the locking device slides into place. A key made from wire bristles is pushed into the holes to open the door. Dogon doors measure about 12 by 16 inches and are often sold at craft markets. Although they are small, they are very heavy.

PHOTOGRAPHY

Bamako is an important center for photography and is well known for its photography workshops and festivals. Notable among these is Africa Photography Encounters, which takes place every two years.

The most famous Malian photographer, Seydou Keïta, was born in Bamako in 1923 and died in 2001. He earned a reputation around the world

A young couple in a photograph taken by Keïta. Keïta was later made the official country photographer of Mali.

for capturing life in his native city. In 1948 working in his tiny studio, he created his own style and documented local people in black-and-white photographs. Although the portraits were posed, they still have a charming and informal feeling to them. People are seen laughing and talking, and wearing their best clothes. But those clothes varied from tribal dress to western business attire, some of it provided by Keïta. Many photographs took elements from both cultures and combined them in a totally new way. Keïta's photographs captured the period during the 1950s and 1960s and earned him his reputation. They are a remarkable record of life in Bamako during that time. In all he left a legacy of 7,000 negatives, the film from which black-and-white prints are made. Keïta's contribution to preserving the art and culture of Mali is enormous because it shows us the point of view of someone who belongs to that culture. In almost all other examples we see Africans through the eyes of westerners. But Keïta was showing us his own people from inside their culture.

EXHIBITION OF PHOTOGRAPHY

The first major exhibition of Keïta's work outside Mali was in 1991 in France. The world suddenly became aware of this remarkable talent and the fascinating people he portrayed. In 2006 the Sean Kelly Gallery in New York showed his work in huge, beautiful black-and-white prints. A foundation in Bamako preserves Keïta's work and allows people to study it. It is called the Seydou Keïta Foundation. Alioune Ba, who was born in Bamako in 1959, is the director of the foundation. He is also a photographer whose work was included in a major exhibition in Washington, D.C., called "Mali, Beyond Timbuktu," in 2006.

YOUNG PHOTOGRAPHERS

Keïta paved the way for a whole generation of African photographers. Two of them from Mali were included in an exhibition called "Snap Judgments: New Positions in Contemporary African Photography" at the International Center of Photography in New York, in 2006. Mohamed Camara was born in Bamako in 1985 and now splits his time between Mali and Paris, a major art center. His work has been shown in exhibitions in several European countries and in Bamako. Sada Tangara was born in Mali in 1984 and now lives in the neighboring country of Senegal. His work has also been seen in many exhibitions, both in Europe and in Africa. They are continuing the tradition of presenting a view of Africa by Africans, not by outsiders.

An image of a Malian gendarme (police officer) taken by Seyou Keïta, one of Mali's most prolific photographers.

LEISURE

FOOTBALL FEVER RUNS HIGH in Mali, as in most nations in Africa and around the world. (Football is the term used throughout most of the world for the game most Americans know as soccer. It is not the same as American football.)

SPORTS

Young boys play in the dusty streets and bare dirt fields, often with a makeshift ball made of rags or newspaper. Mali has fourteen Class A soccer teams. In Bamako, the capital, the football stadium holds 70,000 people. During important matches, such as the qualifying rounds to enter the World Cup, every seat is filled. Mali's national team has become an important contender among African nations. It earned the right to host the 2002 African Cup of Nations tournament, where it took part in the finals. In 2006 Mali took part in the first qualifying round leading up to the 2008 African Cup of Nations, which will take place in Ghana. Then, in 2010, the eyes of the world will be on South Africa which will host the World Cup. It is the first time this event, the most-watched sporting event in the world, will be held on the African continent. Mali is one of three nations in Africa with the greatest number of people taking part in football, in relation to its population.

At the Olympic football tournament in 2004, held in Greece, the Mali Minnows scored a tremendous victory. The team won a game with a 2–0 score over Greece, in Group D. The Mali team had already beaten Cameroon, the 2000 gold medalists during the African qualifying round. Two of the star players were Moussa Coulibaly and Adama Tamboura.

Above: **Soccer is a favorite sport among the young of Mali. Many of them play soccer on makeshift fields like this.**

Opposite: **Malian children play on makeshift swings hung over branches of a tree.**

In an effort to get more Malian children involved in sports and to help them develop better health, a group called RTP (Right To Play) has developed a sports program for children as well as adults. The children, grouped into three sections (under age 10, 10–14, and 15–19) as well as adults over age 20 are brought together to play football and volleyball.

GAMES

The most popular counting game in many parts of Africa is called mancala. It is also known as *oware*, wari, and *bau* in different languages and in different countries. Whatever it is called, it is played the same way. The board is usually made

Another popular variation of soccer is table soccer, also known as foosball.

of wood with little cups or depressions carved out. The players use pebbles, seeds, or any small objects as markers. It is a counting game that is considered as complicated as chess. Players move from one cup to the next, adding and subtracting the markers. Men can be seen playing the game everywhere in Africa. Sometimes they just dig the little hollows in a sandy area and use anything at hand as the playing pieces. One clever man just tore up some bits of orange peel to use instead of seeds. It is considered a game for adults, although children can play it, too.

In the cities of Mali there is a popular game that imitates a football match. In many countries it is called foosball or table soccer. Two players stand on opposite sides of a game table and move carved wooden players attached to poles back and forth, trying to score goals.

FILM

Mali has a small filmmaking industry and has produced some notable films. Among the award-winning Malian filmmakers are Souleymane Cissé, Cheikh Oumar Sissoko, Adama Drabo, Kany Kouyaté, and Abderrahmane Sissako.

In 2006 Sissako wrote and directed a film called *Bamako*. It was a fictional story, but it described many of the issues that concern Mali and Africa today. Much of the film takes place in a courtyard, where people go about their lives, while at the same time a trial is going on involving judges in robes and wigs. There are many stories being told at the same time, and people walk in and out of the courtyard constantly. The film was praised for showing an African story from the viewpoint of the African people.

In Bamako, Malians have a choice of movie houses to go to. Many movies are aimed at the French-speaking population. At the Babemba cinema, for example, people could see the latest Harry Potter film with French subtitles when it was released.

Such leisure activities as going to movies are reserved for those who have enough money to attend—and enough leisure time, too. In Mali, however, leisure time can refer to time spent attending traditional ceremonies, such as weddings and other celebrations. In rural areas, where most Malians live, work consumes so much time, leisure time is a great luxury.

Filmmaker Souleymane Cissé (*right*) with an actress from his film *Waati* at the Cannes Film Festival.

119

FESTIVALS

THE TUAREG ARE SO AT HOME in the Sahara, it is only natural that they would hold their own music festival there. Since 1991 the Festival in the Desert has been held each January, somewhere deep in the Sahara. In recent years, it has been staged in Essakane, a tiny oasis town of a few hundred people located 50 miles (80 km) northwest of Timbuktu. That does not seem like much of a distance, but it takes four hours of hard traveling on sandy dunes and rocky tracks to reach it. All the supplies must be brought in, since there is nothing to buy in the town.

Opposite: **A Tuareg musical group performs at the Festival in the Desert where the best Tuareg musical groups come together.**

Below: **Tuareg riding into Essakane on camels to attend the Festival in the Desert.**

The festival is a true Tuareg event. Everyone stays in tents, just like the Tuareg, and in the evening the temperature can drop nearly to freezing. But the musicians and the audience—most of them Tuareg people—do not seem to mind. This is primarily a music festival, with the best of the Tuareg singers, drummers, and other musicians gathering for a three-day celebration of their culture. It is also the one time of year that families from the most remote parts of the desert meet up and exchange news. The Festival in the Desert is also intended to maintain the Tuareg culture and to help make it part of the world music scene. Western performers share the stage with the native singers, but it is the songs of the Tuareg that take center stage. The best-known Malian guitarist and singer, Ali Farka Touré, performed at the festival in 2003.

While most of the musical performances take place in the evenings, the days are filled with spectacle. Tuareg men race their camels across the desert in a splendid display of riding ability. There are camel parades, crafts shows, and discussions of events affecting the Tuaregs' lives.

Women's groups perform *tinde* music, their traditional singing and drumming, during the daylight hours as well. This is the time for families to visit, drink cups of sweet tea in their tents, and enjoy the traditional Tuareg life.

FESIVAL ON THE NIGER

In 2005 a festival devoted to music, crafts, and cultures began on the Niger River at Ségou. Timed to take advantage of Mali's best weather, this festival, called Festival on the Niger, is held in the beginning of February. The spectacular setting is the backdrop for a cultural festival that includes all of Mali's ethnic groups. The songs and dances of the Fulani, the Bambara, the Songhai, the Dogon, and many more are staged there. The arts and crafts expositions display textiles, pottery, sculpture, and jewelry. Visitors are also treated to puppet shows and pirogue races on the river. In its first two years the audience was mainly Malian, but as the reputation of this festival grows, it is beginning to attract an international audience. It is a rare chance to see so many of Mali's ethnic groups in one place at one time. Even the storytelling of the Dogon is included, something that is rarely seen outside of Dogon Country. Because Ségou is so centrally located and is not far from Bamako, this festival has a chance of becoming the most important cultural event in Mali. And, unlike the Tuareg festival at Essakane, visitors can stay in hotels in Ségou.

Participants in the Festival on the Niger also have a chance to take part in discussions about the ecology of the Niger River and the threats to its future. In addition to celebrating Mali's rich cultural life, the festival gives people a chance to consider Mali's future and the role those cultures will play in that future.

Opposite: **A Dogon dancer. The Festival on the Niger facilitates cultural exchanges between different ethnic groups, such as the Dogon.**

Above: **In Bamako, the festival of Tabaski is celebrated through communal cooking.**

Opposite: **A man wearing a mask. The Bambara and Bozo feel that the masks and puppets allow them to fully express their character's emotions.**

TABASKI

In Mali and in many Muslim countries Ramadan is followed by the celebration of Tabaski, also known as Eid al-adha. This is the most festive and most important holiday of the year for many Muslims. Tabaski celebrates the biblical story of Abraham. Abraham was going to sacrifice his son to obey God's command. Instead, God put a ram in the place of the child. On this day in Mali, Muslims celebrate by slaughtering cattle and sheep. They give away most of the meat to family members, friends, and the poor. They also invite people to their homes to share in a festive meal. To mark the occasion, people get new clothes. In some villages these are sewn by the local tailor. Young girls run excitedly through the village, showing off their new dresses.

The women take the meat from the slaughtered livestock and make stews with sauce and vegetables. These are served with bowls of rice. Villagers visit each other's homes, where they are always offered sweet green tea. Muslims do not drink alcohol, and tea is a favorite drink. During the evening, musicians begin playing their leather drums. They work as a team, creating complicated rhythms. The women and girls dance to the beat of the drums. It is a wonderful celebration and a great break from the daily round of chores.

PUPPET SHOWS

Both the Bambara and the Bozo people stage an annual festival called a masquerade. The people use their puppets and masks to tell a story. The performance usually takes place over a three-day period, with parts of the story being told in the afternoon and at night. Each age group plays a role. The puppets and masks allow the performers to express the characters they represent. By hiding behind the masks and puppets, the people feel free to represent mythical and symbolic creatures. Since the dancers cannot see where they are going, they are guided by a man ringing a little bell. Musicians playing intricate rhythms on their drums accompany the dancers.

For the Malians puppets teach values such as tolerance, peace, and sharing. The puppets also allow things to be said that might be considered too harsh if they came directly from one person to another. They allow Malians to criticize their politicians in a gentler way.

FOOD

MALIANS DO NOT EAT DIFFERENT foods for breakfast, lunch, and dinner as we usually do in the United States. In Mali most meals are made up of a porridge combined with a sauce. Malians have been preparing this dish for hundreds of years. The great traveler Ibn Battuta wrote about eating millet porridge when he visited Mali in 1352! The food does not vary much except for special occasions such as festivals.

There are differences in the foods people eat in different regions of Mali, but some kind of grain is at the center of nearly all dishes. Stews usually combine several grains, such as rice, millet, and sorghum. In the cities rice is the single most important foodstuff, but in the rural areas cereals, millet, and sorghum form the basis of the diet. Couscous is a

Left: **Children performing their daily chore of pounding grain.**

Opposite: **Woman at Mordina market selling produce.**

popular grain. It is made into porridge and then served with a sauce made of fish or meat, if the family can afford it.

Sunday lunch is a special occasion, but only for those who have the money to buy the ingredients. A lunch in Bamako might be a dish made of fish, potatoes, fresh vegetables, and oil. A woman will spend the whole morning preparing this dish for her family. Since most people do not have refrigeration, they can only buy small amounts of fish or meat and must use it quickly.

In the Niger River area, where fish are plentiful during the high-water season, people cook Nile perch, also known as capitaine. The fish can be

A man fishing. Fish is a staple in the Malian diet.

A tea ceremony is a sign of hospitality in Mali and Malians will not refuse tea poured for them by their hosts.

cooked in many ways. It is fried, grilled, or baked, but one of the most popular dishes is a Malian fish stew.

The people of Mali also enjoy three cups of traditional strong, sweet tea. Tea is served in tiny cups and is poured from a teapot at a great height. Serving tea is a very hospitable thing to do, particularly in the Sahara. Each of the three cups represents an aspect of life, and it is not polite to refuse the second and third cups. Drinking hot tea in the hot desert has a way of balancing the heat inside and outside the body. The tea ceremony is also a way to enjoy the environment and to take time to learn about the people of Mali.

Because people eat with their hands, it is very important to observe the local customs. People always eat with their right hands, whether they are right or left handed. This tradition comes from Muslim rules regarding cleanliness and purity.

MALIAN FISH STEW

1 pound dried, salted fish
3 large onions, minced
15–20 okra pods, cooked
4 cups cold water
2 or 3 fresh red chiles, minced (optional)
6 tablespoons vegetable oil
4 tomatoes, diced

Place fish in enough water to cover it, and allow to soak overnight. Then, drain all water and wash off any extra salt. Remove bones. Place fish and 3 cups of the water in a large pan. After water boils, lower the heat and allow fish to simmer.

While fish is simmering, heat oil in a frying pan, and fry half the onions and all the chiles until golden brown. Add tomatoes, and cook for 3 minutes. Stir in rest of water, and continue to simmer for another 15 minutes.

Mix the rest of the onion with okra, and add it to fish. Stir mixture and simmer for about 20 to 30 minutes, until fish softens and the water is reduced a little. Combine the onion, tomato, and chile mixture with the fish.

Serve the stew with rice, dumplings, or any starch preferred.

JOLLOF RICE

Calling this a rice dish may surprise an American cook, since it requires a pound of beef or chicken. To a Malian, however, this is a typical rice dish, full of meat and vegetables.

1 pound lean, boneless beef or chicken
Vegetable oil for frying
2½ cups long-grain white rice
2–3 fresh red chiles, minced
3 tablespoons tomato paste
4 large tomatoes, blanched, peeled, and pureed
    or mashed
Salt and freshly ground white pepper to taste
4 cups stock, or 4 cups water mixed with 3 crushed
    bouillon cubes
4 cloves of garlic, minced
1½ cups diced assorted vegetables, mixed together
    (choose carrots, green beans, mushrooms,
    bell peppers, or any you prefer)
3 large yellow onions, minced
For garnish: 3 hard-boiled eggs, parsley or fresh cilantro, and chopped green-leaf lettuce

Cut beef or chicken into 2-inch cubes or small pieces, and season with salt and pepper.

Cover and let stand for 1 to 2 hours.

Heat vegetable oil in a skillet and brown the meat or chicken pieces. Remove from oil. Pour stock into a large, heavy pan and add meat or chicken pieces. Simmer on low heat until pieces begin to soften, then remove from heat.

Drain the excess oil from the skillet, leaving just enough to fry the onions, garlic, and chiles until golden brown. Add tomatoes, tomato paste, half the vegetable mixture, and 1 cup of stock from the meat or chicken mixture. Stir well, adding salt and pepper to taste. Simmer on low heat for 5 to 7 minutes. Add vegetable sauce to the meat or chicken, and continue to simmer. Stir in rice. Add salt and pepper to taste. Cover and continue to simmer on low heat for about 15 minutes.

Add the remaining vegetables on top of rice, and simmer until the rice absorbs all the stock, softens, and cooks, and the meat or chicken is tender. Additional water may be needed if rice is not fully cooked. Add small amounts, slowly, no more than 1 cup, of lightly salted water as needed.

Serve hot, garnished with lettuce, parsley and hard-boiled eggs.

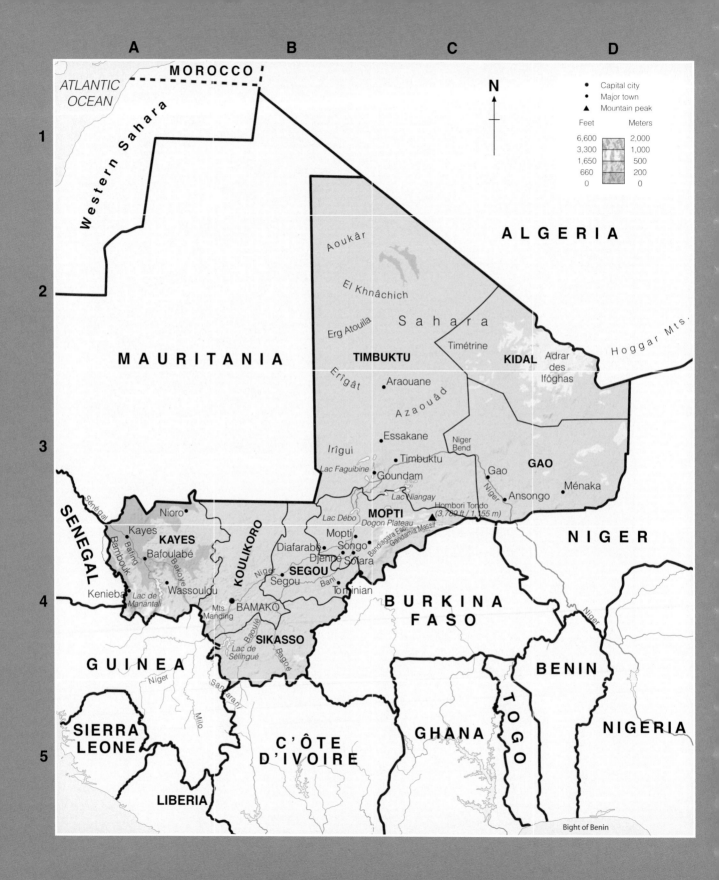

MAP OF MALI

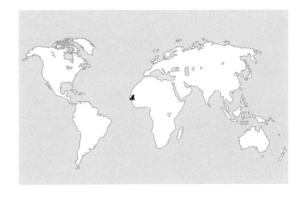

ECONOMIC MALI

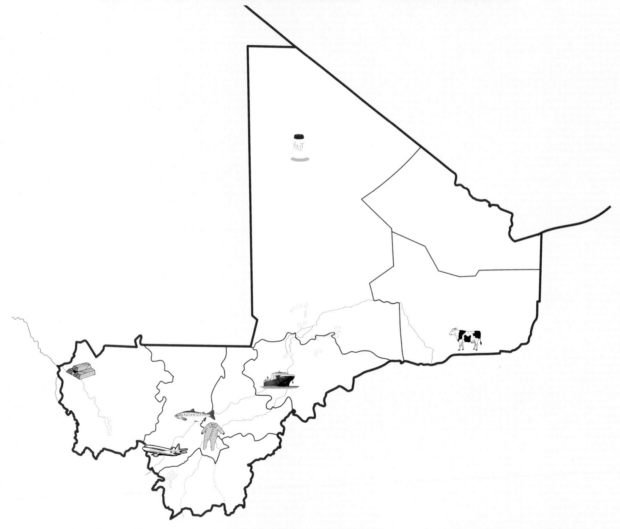

Agriculture	Natural Resources	Services
Cattle	Salt Mines	Port
Cotton	Gold	Airport
	 Fish	

ABOUT
THE ECONOMY

OVERVIEW

Mali is a nation that depends on farming, yet much of its land is not suitable for agriculture. It ranks very low among the nations of the world in its economic development and in all economic statistics. Changes in climate put even greater pressure on farmers. More and more young people are leaving the country to look for work.

GROSS DOMESTIC PRODUCT (GDP)

US $5.433 billion (2005)

WORKFORCE

Agriculture: 70 percent, services 15 percent, industry 15 percent

AGRICULTURAL PRODUCTS

Millet, sorghum, corn, rice, livestock, sugar, cotton, fish, groundnuts

INDUSTRIAL PRODUCTS

Gold

CURRENCY

CFA Franc, pegged to Euro
1 Euro = 656 CFA Francs (2006)
1 USD = 483.88 CFA Francs

EXPORTS

Gold

IMPORTS

petroleum, machinery and equipment, construction materials, foodstuffs, textiles

TRADE PARTNERS

France, Cote d'Ivoire, Belgium, Luxembourg, United States, Germany, Japan

INFLATION RATE

−1.3 percent (2003)

PER CAPITA INCOME

$1,000 (2005)

POPULATION BELOW POVERTY LINE

64 percent

EXTERNAL DEBT

$2.8 billion (2002)

ECONOMIC AID

$596 million (2001) From United States: $44.2 million (2003); also from European Union, France, Canada, China, Netherlands, Germany

MAJOR AIRPORTS

Bamako, Gao, Kayes, Mopti

PORTS

Landlocked; river ports at Mopti, Bamako

CULTURAL MALI

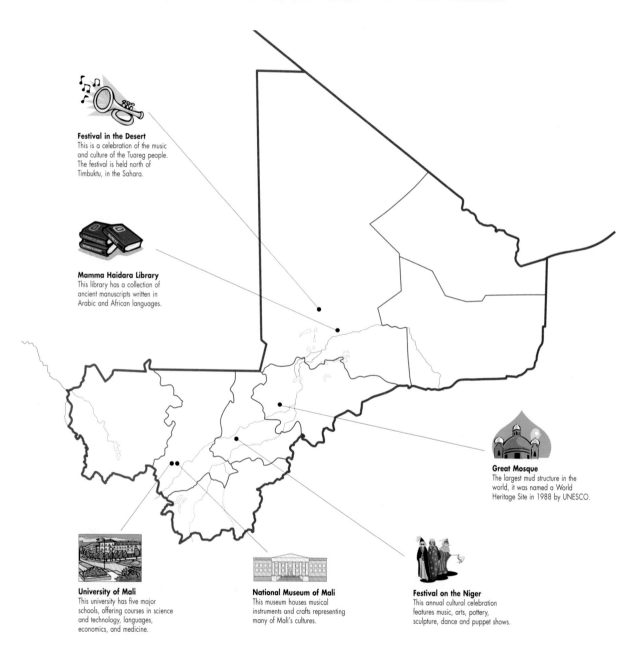

Festival in the Desert
This is a celebration of the music and culture of the Tuareg people. The festival is held north of Timbuktu, in the Sahara.

Mamma Haidara Library
This library has a collection of ancient manuscripts written in Arabic and African languages.

Great Mosque
The largest mud structure in the world, it was named a World Heritage Site in 1988 by UNESCO.

University of Mali
This university has five major schools, offering courses in science and technology, languages, economics, and medicine.

National Museum of Mali
This museum houses musical instruments and crafts representing many of Mali's cultures.

Festival on the Niger
This annual cultural celebration features music, arts, pottery, sculpture, dance and puppet shows.

ABOUT THE CULTURE

OFFICIAL NAME
Republic of Mali

NATIONAL ANTHEM
Seydou Badian Kouyaté, a politican and novelist, composed Mali's national anthem, *Pour l'Afrique et pour toi, Mali* (*For Africa and For You, Mali*).

CAPITAL
Bamako

ADMINISTRATIVE REGIONS
Gao, Kayes, Kidal, Koulikoro, Mopti, Ségou, Sikasso, Timbuktu, capital region (Bamako)

POPULATION
12 million (2006 est.)

LIFE EXPECTANCY AT BIRTH
42 years (2002)

ETHNIC GROUPS
Bambara, Malinke, Fulani, Sarakcole, Songhai, Tuareg, Dogon

LITERACY RATE
Adult: 19 percent

LANGUAGES
French, Bambara

RELIGIONS
Islam 90 percent; Indigenous 6–10 percent; Christian 2–4 percent

NATIONAL HOLIDAYS
January 20 Armed Forces Day; May 1 Labor Day; May 25 Africa Day; September 22 Independence Day

LEADERS IN POLITICS
President Amadou Toumani Touré (1991–92; 2002–)
Prime Minister Ousmane Issoufi Maiga (2004–)

LEADERS IN THE ARTS
Ali Farka Touré, musician
Seydou Keïta, photographer

TIME LINE

IN MALI	IN THE WORLD

200 B.C.
City of Denné-Jeno settled.

4th–8th century
Mali is part of Empire of Ghana.

8th century
Songhai Empire established.

1235
Sundjata Keita, king of Mandinko Kingdom, creates Mali Empire.

1255
Keita dies; Mansa Jurulenko becomes ruler.

1270
Aboubakari I rules until 1285.

1312
Mansa Musa takes over.

1324
Mansa Musa makes pilgrimage to Mecca.

1332
Mansa Musa dies, and Mali Empire begins to decline.

1352
Ibn Battuta visits Mali.

15th century
Mali is ruled by Songhai Empire.

16th century
Songhai Empire collapses.

A.D. 600
Height of Mayan civilization

1000
The Chinese perfect gunpowder and begin to use it in warfare.

1530
Beginning of trans-Atlantic slave trade organized by the Portuguese in Africa.

1558–1603
Reign of Elizabeth I of England

1620
Pilgrims sail the *Mayflower* to America.

1776
U.S. Declaration of Independence

1789–99
The French Revolution

1861
The U.S. Civil War begins.

IN MALI	IN THE WORLD
late 19th century French defeat Malian leaders.	**1869** The Suez Canal is opened.
1904 Mali becomes a French colony.	
1920 Mali becomes part of French Sudan.	**1914** World War I begins.
	1939 World War II begins.
	1945 The United States drops atomic bombs on Hiroshima and Nagasaki.
	1949 The North Atlantic Treaty Organization (NATO) is formed.
1960 Mali becomes independent.	
1960–1968 President Modibo Keita rules.	**1966–69** The Chinese Cultural Revolution
1968 President Keita arrested by Lieutenant Moussa Traoré.	
1980 Mali students begin to organize resistance to military rule.	**1986** Nuclear power disaster at Chernobyl in Ukraine
1991 Violence erupts between people and soldiers at presidential palace; Moussa Traoré arrested by Amadou Toumani Touré.	**1991** Break-up of the Soviet Union
1992 Alpha Omar Konaré becomes president; reelected in 1997.	**1997** Hong Kong is returned to China.
	2001 Terrorists crash planes in New York, Washington, D.C., and Pennsylvania.
2002 Amadou Toumani Touré elected president. Mali hosts African Cup of Nations.	**2003** War in Iraq
2007 Presidential elections held.	

GLOSSARY

Bambara
Also known as Bamana. Mali's largest ethnic group. The Bambara language is spoken by about 80 percent of the people.

Djenné
City that is home to the famous Great Mosque.

Dogon
Cliff-dwelling people whose masked dances are widely known.

harmattan
A fierce wind that blows across the Sahara.

madrassa
A school where Muslim religious education is given.

mancala
A counting game played throughout Africa.

Sahel
The region of semidesert to the south of the Sahara; as the climate changes, more of this land turns to desert.

tagilmust
A headdress made of a long length of cloth that protects the wearer against the fierce harmattan and the sun.

Tuareg
A nomadic people who travel across the Sahara by camel.

FURTHER INFORMATION

BOOKS

Burns, Khephra. *Mansa Musa: The Lion of Mali*. New York: Harcourt, 2001.

Masoff, Joy. *Mali, Land of Gold & Glory*. Waccabuc, New York: Five Ponds Press, 2002.

Supples, Kevin. *Mali*. Washington, DC: National Geographic, 2004.

WEB SITES

Children's Introduction to Mali. http://www.oxfam.org.uk/coolplanet/ontheline/schools/magicmali

Crafts from Mali. http://www.worldcraftsvillage.com/country.asp?name=Mali

Celebrating Tabaski holiday. http://www.peacecorps.gov/kids/like/mali-celebration3.html

Camel trek to Timbuktu. http://www.highonadventure.com/Hoa98dec/Timbuktu/timbuktu.htm

MUSIC

World Music Institute program, Songs of the Desert, Tinariwen, 2006, New York City Program from Festival au Desert, Essakane 2006.

Festival in The Desert, Wrasse Records, 2003, recorded at Essakane, Mali.

Ali Farka Touré, *Savane*, World Circuit Production, Nonesuch Records, Inc., 2006.

Africa: Never Stand Still, 3-disc music package with book, Ellipsis Arts, 1994, Roslyn, NY.

DVDS

Peoples and Cultures of Mali, a musical journey, Tandem Films, Bamako, Mali.

BIBLIOGRAPHY

Blauer, Ettagale. *African Elegance*. New York: Rizzoli International Publishers, 1999.

Else, David, et al. *West Africa*. Hawthorn, Victoria, Australia: Lonely Planet Publications, 1999.

Lauré, Jason and Ettagale Blauer. *Africatrek, An American Photographer's Odyssey in Africa*. iAfrika, 2002.

Seligman, Thomas K. and Kristyne Loughran, editors. *Art of Being Tuareg*. Los Angeles: UCLA Fowler Museum of Cultural History, 2006.

Velton, Ross. Mali: *The Bradt Travel Guide*, Second Edition. Guilford, CT: Globe Pequot Press Inc., 2004

Andriamirado, Sennen, and Virginie Andriamirado. *Mali Today*. Paris, France: Les Editions du Jaguar, 1997.

Davis, Shawn R. *Dogon Funerals*. Photo Essay, African Arts, Summer 2002.

Dogon funeral rituals. Personal commentary from Victor Englebert, Assou Sagara, Ibrahim Ag Alhabib, Richard Meyer, and Karen Booth.

National Geographic Map: Soccer Unites the World, 2006.

National Geographic Map: Africa Today, 2001.

Michelin Map: Africa North and West, 1996.

Coetzee, Toast. "So, I went to Timbuktu the other day . . ." Go! Magazine, August 2006.

Roberts, David and José Azel. Below the Cliff of Tombs, Mali's Dogon, National Geographic Magazine, October 1990.

http://www.aaas.org/international/ehn/waterpop/mali.htm
http://www.infoplease.com
http://www.vmfa.state.va.us/mali
http://www.fao.org/ag/agp/agpc/doc/Counprof/Mali
www.eshop.africa.com
http://www.africaguide.com/country/mali/culture.htm
http://www.npr.org/programs/re/archivesdate/2003/may/mali
http://www.nytimes.com/2005/09/11/international/africa/11mali.html
http://mali.pwnet.org/history/history_mali_empire.html
http://www.aol.svc.worldbook.aol.com/wb/Article?id=ar340220
http://www.bbc.co.uk/worldservice/africa/features/storyofAfrica/
http://www.everyculture.com/Ja-Ma/Mali.html
http://dispatchesfromthevanishingworld.com/dispatch31/printerd31.html
http://www.africa-ata.org/mali.htm
http://www.historycentral.com/NationbyNation/Mali/Population.html
http://www.metmuseum.org/toah/hd/gld/hd_gold.htm
http://www.afrol.com/News2001/mal002_desertification.htm
http://www.fordfound.org/publications/ff_report/view_ff-report_detailcfm?report_index=4
http://www.risc.org.uk/bogolan/index.htm
http://international.loc.gov/intldl/malihtml/about.html
http://www.fao.org/docre/W4347E/w4347e0i.htm
http://www.merck.com/cr/enabling_access/developing_world/mectizan/
http://www.sfusd.k12.ca.us/schwww/sch618/Ibn_Battuta/

INDEX